Living the Vanlife

Living the Vanlife

ON THE ROAD TOWARD SUSTAINABILITY,
COMMUNITY & JOY

NOAMI J. GREVEMBERG

SIMON ELEMENT
NEW YORK   LONDON   TORONTO   SYDNEY   NEW DELHI

SIMON
ELEMENT

An Imprint of Simon & Schuster, Inc.
1230 Avenue of the Americas
New York, NY 10020

First Simon Element hardcover edition July 2023

SIMON ELEMENT is a trademark of Simon & Schuster, Inc.

For information about special discounts for bulk purchases, please contact Simon & Schuster Special Sales at 1-866-506-1949 or business@simonandschuster.com.

The Simon & Schuster Speakers Bureau can bring authors to your live event. For more information or to book an event, contact the Simon & Schuster Speakers Bureau at 1-866-248-3049 or visit our website at www.simonspeakers.com.

Interior design by Matt Ryan

Manufactured in China

10 9 8 7 6 5 4 3 2 1

Library of Congress Cataloging-in-Publication Data has been applied for.

ISBN 978-1-9821-7961-8
ISBN 978-1-9821-7962-5 (ebook)

To my sweet, precious loves:
my niece, Jeannine, and nephews,
Kael and Jeriah.

You are each a bright light in my life.

May you stay ever curious and
fly toward your dreams.

Contents

Foreword

Across the landscapes and seascapes of our
lives, we encounter places, experiences,
and souls that challenge and inspire us to
grow and shift with the seasons. This is not
anything new. As the work of Octavia E. Butler
and her subsequent lineage teaches us:

All that you touch
you change
all that you change
changes you
the only lasting truth is change
god is change.[1]

One such soul who has touched
and changed the trail of this
wandering spirit's trajectory is Noami.

WHEN NOAMI MESSAGED ME recently and said she and Dustin were camped out in Knik and could be in town in an hour to meet up, I was elated. In my mind, I saw them waking up under the protection of the late-summer Chugach Mountains to the greeting of glacier-fed water's song, feeling the magnitude of the Matanuska-Susitna Valley. I envisioned Irie rolling over the silt and gravel of the river flats before making her way down the final stretch of the Glenn Highway into Dgheyay Kaq'.[2] The thought stirred memories of my own camping trips in this area and brought a smile to my lips. I texted Noami to meet me at the Rustic Goat, a favorite local restaurant, as I hopped into my Toyota Sienna to run a few errands before heading east.

IN OCTOBER 2019, I attended my first vanlife gathering hosted by Women on the Road (WOTR) on Núu-agha-tʉvʉ-pʉ/Diné Bikéyah in what is known as Moab, Utah.[3] I had been invited by Jaylyn Gough, founder of Native Women's Wilderness, to offer a land acknowledgment to open the weekend. There were a few folx from social media that I hoped would be there, and Noami was one of them. We first "met" through Instagram before the shopping button was an option and just as influencing was starting to take off in the outdoor industry. I remember stumbling on @irietoaurora's page for the first time and thinking, *Damn, there are other BIPOC out here doing vanlife and THRIVING?!* As a queer Deg Xit'an Dene and Sugpiaq femme person from Alaska who has been on and off the road since 2014, I,

like many others, had predominantly witnessed and met white cis-heteronormative people engaged in this life. I had slid into Noami's DMs only a month prior to the WOTR gathering in response to her call for accountability in the vanlife community. Her words resonated with me, as I had just traveled through so-called Canada along the Highway of Tears and was feeling frustrated by the lack of real conversations regarding the safety of BIPOC on the road.[4] Although our paths did not cross during this gathering, as Noami and Dustin were in Louisiana for another event, the connection had been made, and my exposure to one #vanlife community space only solidified my desire to see more diversity and inclusion.

When Noami launched Diversify Vanlife, a platform that was desperately needed to change the narrative of who belonged on the road, a massive shift in #vanlife began to happen. The space offered accessible and approachable resources for getting started and building community from BIPOC perspectives. Our community of nomads and part-time travelers grew in beautiful ways as folx began to see one another and our stories reflected in the mainstream narrative. Works like the *Green Book*,[5] which traced the movement of Black people, were elevated, and the *Women on the Road* podcast passed the mic to Diversify Vanlife's podcast *Nomads at the Intersections*. It finally felt as though there was space to discuss issues such as missing and murdered Indigenous people at their intersection with vanlife that wasn't just shouting into the void. This shift felt like the transition we needed. Diversify Vanlife was change.

THE WOTR GATHERING was one of the last major group events that I participated in before the first strain of the coronavirus swept through the world. Two years later, in the summer of 2021, Alaska began welcoming the waves of visitors knocking on its doors. The imperially imposed border between the United States and Canada began to crack open as the State of Alaska's economy craved tourism. This opening created an avenue for people to travel across Lingít Aaní and Dënéndeh by train and car, while planes brought people by air with cheap tickets and airline subsidies.[6] As a formerly more involved Instagram member, I watched as many of my connections, specifically in the outdoor industry, made their way north to visit the homelands of my peoples, though many of our villages and small towns remained on lockdown.

You see, Alaska has this allure for people, this draw that calls to the spirits of those seeking a dream of the "last frontier," of freedom to roam, and to see large animals that have mostly been pushed out of their lands across the contiguous United States. Using its promise of resource wealth, the state also draws people here to work in tourism, oil and gas, fisheries, health care, and several other industries. As an Indigenous person of this Nuna,[7] I have seen and welcomed guests as a cultural interpreter, café barista, and raft guide in Denali National Park, and have interacted with several visitors engaged in the commercial fishing industry in Bristol Bay. It's always striking to see the way people approach and react to the variety of ecosystems across this vast state. Even more striking is the acknowledgment—or lack thereof—that these are indeed Indigenous lands.

Though the outdoor industry community had been becoming more aware of how to engage in ethical and responsible ways on native lands thanks to the work of many Indigenous activists and allies, what I witnessed was that much of the talk happening in social media spaces did not translate to action as Alaska became a destination for early pandemic travel. It was disappointing and hurtful to see folx visit for photo shoots and projects, flying into Alaska for a week, accessing the land and waters that many of our own people still struggle to find the resources to access, then flying out to launch a campaign by some brand that highlighted their trip. Where was the intention? Where was the outreach to those of us who called this place home? Where was the relationship?

HER CREAM-COLORED EXTERIOR peeked out from behind the corner of the Rustic Goat, and my stomach fluttered a little. Here we were, a few years down the road from our initial internet connection, meeting up in person in Dgheyay Kaq'. After a summer spent on a commercial fishing boat in Bristol Bay and pulling back from social media, I welcomed and was excited for the opportunity to connect with Noami, Dustin, Amara, and Irie. I parked my Sienna next to Irie and found them sitting upstairs looking over the menu. For the next couple of hours or so, we visited and laughed over food as our ancestors and peoples have done since time immemorial. In person, I finally heard the story behind the Aurora in @irietoaurora and understood. The pull of the northern lights had drawn Noami and Dustin here to the north. Like so many others before them, Alaska had called, and they answered the song of the land to travel north for a season of summer harvest. It felt like I had known Noami long before this, and she fit right into Alaska, complete with Xtratufs and all.

Living the Vanlife can—in collaboration with emergent strategy, radical joy, radical imagination, action, and rest—help us build and restore communities of reciprocity in an ever-shifting, ever-changing world where climate change and migration and resource overconsumption all challenge outdated visions of the "American Dream."[8] Before the imposition of colonialism, our peoples moved freely with the land and the animals that called it home. We were and are part of the cycles of the seasons, moving with the fish and caribou to berry and medicine patches. We are often accompanied by motorized vehicles, ATVs, and snowmobiles as we adapt to shorter periods of time in a mixed cash economy and climate change. Vanlife, when practiced in a responsible and ethical way, creates what Leanne Betasamosake Simpson calls "flight paths out of settler colonialism."[9] By engaging in the time-honored tradition of storytelling, understanding how to build relationships with brands that are in alignment with their values, and living life to the fullest while moving with intention on the road, I believe Noami, Dustin, Amara, and Irie have shown us one such flight path out of settler colonialism. As you read or listen to this book, I hope you take the time to meditate on slow travel, minimalism, and the tools that Noami effortlessly weaves into her story to find your own balance of integrity, reciprocity, and relation while traveling across this Indigenous land.

FOREWORD ENDNOTES

1   Octavia Estelle Butler and N. K. Jemisin, *Parable of the Sower* (New York: Grand Central Publishing, 2019).

2   Dgheyay Kaq' is the name for the area known as Anchorage in Dena'ina Ełnena, or the Lands and Waters of the Dena'ina Dene Peoples.

3   The Women on the Road gathering was brought together by the creators of *Women on the Road*, a podcast and gathering space previously hosted by Laura Borichevsky, who now curates *Sex Outside* with *She Explores*'s Gale Straub, Ravel Media cofounder Hailey Hirst, and Noël Russell.

4   Highway 16, also known as the Highway of Tears, runs from Prince Rupert to Prince George. Many Indigenous women and girls have gone missing and/or been murdered along this highway. In 2019, while traveling down from Alaska to the lower forty-eight, I unexpectedly found myself alone on this highway and had to confront at a deep level what it meant to travel and live solo as a queer, Indigenous femme person. For more information on Missing and Murdered Indigenous Relations (MMIR) and the movement to stop these crimes, please read *Reclaiming Power and Place: The Final Report of the National Inquiry into Missing and Murdered Indigenous Women and Girls* and watch the documentary *Sisters Rising* at https://www.sistersrisingmovie.com/. To read a long-form article on Highway 16, check out Al Jazeera's 2021 piece "The Stench of Death on Canada's Highway of Tears" by Brandi Morin.

5   *The Negro Motorist Green Book* by Victor Hugo Green was first published in 1936 and shared safe places for Black people to eat and stay across America while on the road during the Jim Crow era.

6   "Crippled Airline Industry to Get $25 Billion Bailout, Part of It as Loans," *New York Times*, March 17, 2021, https://www.nytimes.com/2020/04/14/business/coronavirus-airlines-bailout-treasury-department.html.

7   Nuna = root of land across Inuit language families.

8   We have adrienne maree brown and her love affair with the work of Octavia E. Butler and Grace Lee Boggs to thank for this framework, which she pulled down to earth for us. "Emergent Strategy is a humble philosophy, a way to acknowledge the real power of change, and be in the right relationship to it. Its intent is to deepen relationships, build trust, and political alignment. Emergent Strategy practices strengthen imagination and the capacity to think beyond the limitations of socialization—beyond competition, beyond binaries, and beyond linear, short-term outcomes" (see the Emergent Strategy Ideation Institute home page at https://esii.org). For the emergent strategy framework, please read *Emergent Strategy: Shaping Change, Changing Worlds* by adrienne maree brown.

9   Leanne Betasamosake Simpson, *As We Have Always Done* (Minneapolis: University of Minnesota Press, 2017).

dear Sister from the Southeast Isles
it is 2:17 on a Saturday night in
    Dena'ina Ełnena.
you have traveled these back roads
highways, country lanes, dirt drives
to this northern land
to heed the calling of some sort of
    ancestral knowledge

crossing over the lands, rivers, lakes,
    valleys, canyons
creek beds cradling salmon, streams of
    silvers and sockeye
you say
my People are Fish People too
we smile because we know
Truth even before our eyes laid on
    each other
when our voices met
somewhere on the
trails of the before times

you came to see the aurora
Ancestors of the north
they sang you here to this place
we call home
so that you would know how to find
    your way back
when the floods come and
    the seas rise

67, 68, 69, 70
heart stop, heatstroke,
drought, monsoon
the breath in between
this is the transition
for better or worse
we wash our single pot and release
    gray water
into the gardens along the roadside
waiting for the dandelions
    to grow out of
plastic water bottles and
    aluminum cans

follow the lichens
    and mosses
give your gifts of offering
to the trail of water
    and land
from the bayous and estuaries
to the Northern Lights
home to the Salmon People

—Deenaalee Hodgdon,
Deg Xit'an Dene & Sugpiaq,
executive director of On the Land Media
Summer 2022

Welcome to Vanlife

I stood terrified, thinking to myself, *Is this what my life has come to—pooping in a hole outdoors?*

Once upon a time I wanted a big house with a walk-in closet and my own bathroom, complete with a soaking tub, rain shower, and a comfy toilet seat. And for a while, I chased after that dream with vigor and verve. In fact, if anyone had even suggested that I would one day forgo these luxuries and live in a van, I would have laughed outright. But there, with the sounds of the forest around me, I squatted, exposed and vulnerable like never before.

My partner and I were about a month into vanlife and, up to this point, I had managed to avoid the unmentionable transaction. As I discovered, it's not very hard to find public restrooms in the US. And during that first month on the road, we were zipping across the country, along highways and interstates dotted with truck stops, rest areas, and visitor centers. Even though I knew the inevitable moment would come, the mere thought of it brought on heaps of anxiety. But as I perched into position and exhaled with a sigh, my gaze was drawn to the captivating setting before me—the hazy peaks of the Blue Ridge Mountains stretching across the landscape, flanked by a lush green valley. The view calmed me. And at that moment, I realized that pooping outdoors ain't half bad.

But in all seriousness, this daring act gave way to an undeniable freedom. It's still not without unpleasantness, but it's far from the most uncomfortable or challenging aspects I've faced on my vanlife journey. Although I now relish a way of life that pushes me out of my comfort zone and inspires me to discover the things that bring me joy, for most of my adult life I was afraid to make sacrifices and take risks. I started with nothing, and I had worked hard to get where I was. And like most thirtysomethings around me, I was convinced that I was traveling on the right path.

Then, in 2016, I was hit with a realization that forced me to question where my life was going and ultimately led me to embrace an unconventional life in a van on the road. Before this time, I had been going through the motions of daily life, sabotaging any goals or aspirations I set for myself. I had been struggling to prioritize my own needs, perpetuating unhealthy habits and behaviors. Above all, I had lost touch with my values,

the consequences of which often left me in a haze of inauthenticity. It was a pivotal moment of self-acceptance. The painful truth I had to come to terms with was that the life I had been working to create no longer served the person I wanted to be.

That first year on the road, I dared not look back. Instead, I ran toward change. It was an emotional odyssey that tested my resolve at every turn. From the distress of abandoning my previously established life plan and sense of security, to the unpredictability and physical discomforts of adapting to a tiny life on the road, as well as the unexpected criticism and backlash from my peers—it all left me feeling isolated, alone, and uncertain. Those early struggles served as an initiation that compelled me to explore deeper into my desires, dreams, thoughts, and behaviors. With this awareness, I dared to commit myself to a more authentic and intentional way of life.

Vanlife has grown in popularity in recent years, and like many other alternative lifestyles, including minimalism, tiny living, and the eco movements, to name a few, the narrative has often been constructed to appear synonymous with consumerism. The fixation on high-end vans and expensive custom buildouts with all the bells and whistles and the thousands of articles and videos online selling everything you need to *live your best vanlife* are overwhelming and can make this lifestyle seem unattainable. So it's easy to understand why many may feel discouraged.

But as you'll learn in the pages ahead, this does not have to be the case. I believe vanlife is about intentional living, and although it seems like an intimidating process, getting started in vanlife can be quite simple. I truly believe that vanlife is and should be attainable for anyone who wants to live it. And that includes you!

I've had an incredible range of experiences on the road, including experimenting with passions, learning new skills, and finding ways to achieve financial freedom by doing things that I enjoy. By shifting away from traditional markers of success, I have removed limitations on what or how my life can be. Likewise, fulfilling my childhood dream of travel has empowered me to move beyond the idea of a "bucket list." I've learned a lot through the many trials and errors, and failures and successes. This is why I feel confident in serving as your resource.

My intention for this book is to help you on your journey into vanlife. Perhaps you're curious but don't know how to get started. Or maybe you've already established a life on the road but need help adjusting. Or you're a seeker, looking for an alternative life beyond the confines of the traditional societal road map. Within these pages, you'll find tools to help you understand what you need to begin and thrive on your road life journey. Because anyone can live this lifestyle. Yes, anyone.

Even years in, my vanlife journey continues to present many *aha* moments and windows of opportunity where I can live in alignment with my truth. As a Black-identifying, mixed-race, queer immigrant in a lifestyle that is predominantly white, I have been challenged to step into my power as an active leader. In 2019, I founded Diversify Vanlife, a growing community orga-

nization facilitating representation for Black, Indigenous, Asian, LatinX, and other people of color (BIPOC) within the vanlife community. I'm proud of the continued work that is being done in this space. And this book is a contribution to that purpose, written through the lens of the multiple intersections that I navigate.

Without a doubt, these intersections have been instrumental to how I experience life on the road. The truth is, the narrative of mainstream vanlife has failed to include the spectrum of marginalized voices, which plays a direct role in the BIPOC community's apprehension toward this lifestyle. So, throughout this book, I will address specific concerns, questions, and needs related to the unique experiences of BIPOC road travelers. Because we deserve the opportunity to experience the freedoms and benefits of vanlife. Because we deserve to take up space!

My hope is that others will use this information to build understanding and empathy and examine ways to help create change for a more equitable community and world. We're all on our own paths, but the destination is the same—to become the best versions of ourselves.

Breathe easy, friends. Yes, this book is about vanlife. But it goes beyond the superficial and touches on the multifaceted aspects of this lifestyle that can easily go unaddressed but that have a big impact. This book is for anyone who bucks the norm and challenges the status quo.

Welcome to your journey! And what a beautiful journey it will be. Enjoy the ride!

CHAPTER 1

How I Ended Up
Living in a Van

Since we're embarking on this new and exciting journey together, I'd like to start by sharing my backstory, so you can get to know a little about me, your vanlife guide.

GROWING UP IN TRINIDAD: MY VILLAGE LIFE

I grew up in a small fishing village on the island of Trinidad in the West Indies. My childhood home was a humble two-bedroom, cookie-cutter concrete-block house with green shutters and was nestled in a tiny village in a humid rainforest that was just a few miles from the beach. It was an upbringing that would feel otherworldly to most Americans. My dad spent his days toiling away at labor-intensive jobs for an oil company, and my mom worked as a maid and sometimes as a food vendor for extra money to make ends meet. But what we lacked in financial resources we gained back in an abundance of splendor, surrounded by endless natural beauty.

As a child, I spent my days swimming in waterfalls, fishing in the rivers, foraging for food, and running barefoot in the forest—I don't remember a time growing up when my mom wasn't yelling at me to put on shoes. I needed to feel the earth between my toes back then in much the

same way as I still do now. I went to sleep each night to an orchestra of insects churring and bullfrogs bellowing, and I awoke each morning to a concert of birds singing and monkeys howling in my backyard. A love and appreciation for nature has always been a part of my spirit.

We never took vacations as a family, so during the long August break from school, my brothers and I would pass the days exploring our forest playground. The deep-green sea of life seemed to go on forever. Rays of mellow sunlight filtered through the dense canopy, illuminating the leaves in an unearthly green-gold luminescence. We would stand in awe looking up at these mighty ancient giants as they disappeared into the sky. Hours passed as we twirled around searching for the colorful birds and primates that sang sweetly. My forest was alive and astir with life.

Throughout childhood, nature was my place of respite. I was fifteen when my parents split up, after which the forest became my reprieve from the grief of loss. In this world, I was able to be fully present; closely observing the ebbs and flows of nature helped me to understand that a big part of life is death in all its forms. The connection I built with death at this young age helped me to come to terms with loss in my own life and prepared me in ways I didn't know then for my life and journey in the outdoors.

COMING TO AMERICA

There were no opportunities for a young girl like me in Trinidad: no college, no career in my future. My father is a descendant of enslaved Africans, and my mother traces her lineage from indentured laborers who came from East India; this is a background that we share with a majority of our compatriots. The effects of our colonial history have left their mark on the people of Trinidad, creating a cycle of oppression and poverty that is difficult to escape. And while Trinidad is a country rich in natural resources, lack of access to education, lack of opportunities, and the effects of oppressive imperialism have left many families shackled by the weight of poverty. My life was no different.

My parents split shortly before my senior year of high school; the adversity that plagued our poverty-stricken family life got the best of them. I was determined to break those chains. In my last year of high school, I saved every dollar I earned to pay for a visa application. And the day I graduated, at age sixteen, I called the American Embassy in Port of Spain. Two months later, I took my first airplane flight to the US—with a broken-down suitcase, an empty wallet, and a big ol' American Dream.

After landing at JFK, I got my first taste of the concrete jungle of America, a daunting experience compared to the sheltered life in my village. The bustling streets, the lights, the sounds, the smells, the people, the trains and cabs, the clothes, and a new way of life; I was bewitched by it! I wanted to be like one of those striking women in New York City with the stilettos and pencil-skirt suit, always in a hurry with a bagel and coffee in hand. I used to imagine they were running off to live their own American Dream—a successful career, financial stability, maybe a house with a white picket fence.

I lived in Brooklyn for a couple of months. I'd take the train to my job at a hardware store every day where I made less than minimum wage. I was grateful, but my dream of moving up in the world was too big. Many evenings after work I'd hop on the train to Penn Station, grab an Auntie Anne's pretzel, and lose myself, walking down Fifth Avenue to the East Village and dreaming of a glamorous life like I imagined one of the strangers on their phones sitting outside a fancy café had. *One day*, I thought, *that will be me.*

And I put myself right on the path to getting there. The hectic, congested life in New York City proved to be more than I had bargained for. As an Afro-Indo immigrant, opportunities for jobs and housing were competitive, and the cost of living coupled with the fast pace made me feel like I was running on a hamster wheel. Shortly after acquiring my green card, I moved to Louisiana, a place I had visited a few times since coming to the US. The slower way of life and the warmer climate gave me the space to find my bearings. I entered

college at twenty-five, an adult student. I decided to register at a local community college in Baton Rouge, where I fell in love with environmental studies. I earned an associate's degree in technical science, which gave me the tools to find a job in my field, kick-starting my career.

I went on to pursue a bachelor's degree in coastal science at the University of New Orleans. The knowledge and technical skills I acquired in my courses opened doors to opportunities I had only dreamt of. My job allowed me to work outdoors in the swamps and marshes of the Gulf Coast. Every day I'd board an airboat or skiff and navigate canals and bayous, dredging through murky water of dirt and mud and passing the occasional friendly cottonmouth snake. It was freeing. Being able to watch the brilliant, golden sunrise dance on the calm water each morning made it even better.

Despite the joy I felt, it wasn't the easiest period of my life. I worked two jobs while in school, the second being a nighttime bartending gig. And as much as I enjoyed my classes, college was hard. My full course load and busy work schedule caused me to miss out on the typical social college experience. But one of the best things about going back to school as an adult was my greater sense of purpose and drive. Though I could still live without the trauma of algebra, college put me one step closer to that American Dream, which I craved achieving more than anything else. As evidence that I was on the right path, I became the first person in my family to attend college and earn a degree.

I met my husband, Dustin, during my last year of college, as we continued to pursue our careers.

I landed a job as an environmental scientist during my senior year, which I continued for a while after earning my degree. Dustin started working as a project engineer for a commercial construction company right after graduation. We were on the path that society said was correct, so this was surely the path to fulfilling our dreams, right? Yet, with every step, I felt further from that feeling of wholeness, of having it all figured out.

OUR VANLIFE LOVE STORY

Before moving on, I want to share the story of how Dustin and I met and became a vanlife couple. It was our senior year in college. He went to Louisiana State University, and I attended the University of New Orleans. LSU football season was in full swing, and a girlfriend invited me to go tailgating with her. I had just broken up with my then boyfriend and was more inclined to stay in bed and weep. But on this warm summer day, she was determined to get me out of my dark and gloomy town house.

When we got to campus, the ripping of the drumline and the vibrations deep in my chest pulled me right out of my funk. We parked at the edge of campus and took a long walk to her friend's tailgate party. It was about noon and by the time we made it there, I was drenched in sweat and my curls had consumed all the 90 percent humidity in the air.

We were greeted by a friendly group of LSU fans, who were grilling and dancing. I indulged in cheap beer and interesting conversation. It wasn't long before I was approached by a kind, clean-faced fellow with a southern accent and the charm to match. I was smitten. We spent the next twelve hours locked in conversation, bonding over our love for Johnny Cash and the Doors and all the reasons why Jimi Hendrix is the greatest guitarist of all time. We talked about our fears, our hopes and dreams, our love for Cajun food. And we bonded over our shared love for the outdoors. I went on and on about my dream of seeing America in a van and visiting all sixty-three national parks. He indulged me. Little did we know our lives would align on that very hot summer day in Baton Rouge.

Fast-forward three years later, and Dustin proposed to me during a backpacking trip on the Appalachian Trail. We were married the following year under a cypress tree on the bayou, a fiery Trinidadian girl and a charming southern boy.

HOMELIFE AND THE DAILY GRIND

A couple of years passed after Dustin and I were wed, and our careers progressed as we both moved on to other companies. I went to work in the private sector in Baton Rouge, an hour away from where we lived, and Dustin took a project manager position at a construction company an hour in the opposite direction. We were climbing the corporate ladder and our lives were progressing in the usual manner. Conversations of buying our first home and having a child became more serious. But the new job and change of scenery didn't bring the fulfillment I had hoped for. In fact, a little voice inside asking if there was more only became louder, and I questioned where my life was going. Navigating my new workplace became a challenge, as I

Williamson Photography.

was the only Black woman in an office dominated by white men. Over the course of a few months, I fell into extreme anxiety and depression. The daily two-hour commute only added fuel to the fire.

I spent many days crying in traffic on my way home from the office, wondering if this was what I had to look forward to for the rest of my life. The monotony was soul-sucking. Work, home, party; eat, drink, repeat; day in, day out. I was burnt-out and unfulfilled. Lost. At least my job title made me feel important. When someone would ask me my profession, I'd proudly state, "I'm an environmental scientist." Deep down, though, it meant nothing. I wasn't living up to my full potential. I considered going back to school or starting a business, but neither of those felt right. I was desperate. I knew something would have to change, but I didn't know what or how. At that point, feeling stuck was an understatement. Alcohol and parties were a reprieve from the anxiety and fire brewing inside me, but those too became stale. And toxic friendships were frequently the norm of my social life. Was this the American Dream I had so eagerly bought into? All this questioning would eventually lead to our rethinking our very mode of living, to consider giving it all up and trying a completely different way of life, one that had only ever seemed like a figment of our imaginations before: living in a van.

DIGGING UP AN OLD DREAM & SAYING YES TO VANLIFE

I sought refuge in nature during this period, just as I had as a little girl. Being outside was all I could think about. I found inspiration in outdoor pages on Facebook and dreamed of strapping on a pack and hitting the trail. So Dustin and I decided to give it a try. We bought our first hiking backpacks from a discount site for forty dollars each. Mine was blue with an external metal frame that squeezed every part of my core when I wore it. It looked like something you'd see in those old Patagonia photos of adventurers from the 1940s—awkward, bulky, and utterly ridiculous. We planned our first backpacking trip in the Great Smoky Mountains via the Appalachian Trail—five days of hiking and road-tripping. We were stoked!

The morning we got to the trailhead we were in awe, seeing throngs of outdoorists everywhere. We had our permits in hand and were ready to hit the trail. Other hikers of all ages, equipped with giant packs and a keen sense of determination, were heading out on multiday adventures, and they all looked so professional. We were amateurs, and we looked like it too. Not to mention that I was the only Black person I'd seen the entire trip. But I didn't care, because at that moment, I felt unstoppable.

Something shifted in me on that trip, and I have never been the same since. From that point on, I would escape to the mountains every chance I got, despite the fact that it was an undertaking to get there. The nearest mountains were in northern Georgia, about eight hours' drive from New Orleans. These giants are home to the southern terminus of the Appalachian Trail, a place where I started spending all my free time. One day on the trail I ran into a man wearing a tool belt and carrying a pickax over his shoulder. He said he was a trail builder. His description of the job, spending weeks at a time in the backcountry with like-minded people, constructing and repairing trails in scenic locations, and using classic tools like sledgehammers, axes, and chainsaws, was all I needed to hear. When I got home, I signed up to volunteer with a trail crew on the AT. The next season I did my first two weeks building trails in Virginia. The work was physically demanding, and I was the only BIPOC on the team, but I loved it.

It soon became evident that one or two weeks in the mountains were not enough to satisfy my wanderlust. So in the late summer of 2015, Dustin and I took a month off work and road-tripped through California. It was our first time on the West Coast of North America. We traveled through Yosemite National Park and up Highway 1 into the redwoods in a compact rental car. One night while camping in the Avenue of the Giants, it stormed, and we were drenched thanks to a hole in our discount-brand tent. We ended up cuddled in a corner of the car, shivering from the cold, eating stale bread and cheese as we waited for the downpour to pass.

We quickly figured out that the learning curve for road-tripping was steep and expensive, so we made do with what we had: our giant cooler, which took up the entire back seat, and cheap, bulky gear. But we felt free. I was happier than ever to be on the road and out in nature. Little did I know that this would be the trip that pushed us to the other side.

Our vanlife journey started in New Orleans, a city Dustin and I had called home for more than five years. It was the longest I'd stayed in one place since moving to America. If you know anything about New Orleans, you might know it's a place that people are ecstatic to move to, even if that means packing up their whole lives after just one visit. The food, the culture, the music, the people—the birthplace of jazz has it all and never disappoints. New Orleans is a city where you never feel alone. But what I love most about it is the down-home vibe that reminds me of my country. After all, they say New Orleans is the northernmost city in the Caribbean.

To me, New Orleans is the greatest city in the world—and trust me, I've been around. So leaving was no easy decision. I was torn, caught between the pull of this gritty city and the desire to shift my life's trajectory. What made it even harder was that we literally knew no one who had done what we were about to do—disrupting our comfortable lives for the unknown, vagabond life: vanlife.

It was early spring, our favorite time of year. The city was alive with music, preparations were being made for the upcoming festival season, and the sweet smell of magnolias filled the air. But my heart was heavy. I couldn't seem to find joy in anything. My anxiety was through the roof and I was suffering in silence.

I decided to propose an idea to Dustin, an old dream we had shared years earlier, a dream that got buried in the noise of other people's ideas of what life should be. One evening I got home early from work, prepared a nice dinner, and waited for him to arrive. He came in and made his way to the kitchen, where I stood with nerves on edge. "I have something to tell you," I blurted out.

"Me too," he said in a shaky voice. "I have something I want to ask you."

After a long back-and-forth about who should go first, I got up the nerve. "Remember that thing we talked about, getting a van and traveling the country?"

"Yeah," he said, in an anxious tone, a grin growing on his face.

"I think we should do it," I said.

"I was going to say the same thing," Dustin exclaimed as he scooped me up and twirled me around the room. It seemed we had come to the decision separately, at the same time. Serendipitous, don't you think?

You see, deciding to uproot your entire life and give up everything you've worked for to go against the grain is no easy thing, especially when you need your partner to be on board. There we were, two scared thirtysomethings, about to take a giant leap into the unknown.

When we announced to our friends and loved ones that we were leaving New Orleans to travel the country in a van, it was not received in the celebratory way we had imagined. We learned right away that one of the greatest tests of choosing this alternative lifestyle is realizing that when you decide to go against the grain, you sometimes must stand alone. It was a radical shift that many of our friends just couldn't get behind. And it was a hard lesson, learning that there will always be people who will question your motives, who will doubt you, who won't accept you or support you.

Some people will never see the dream, so you might as well do it anyway.

SEARCHING FOR OUR DREAM RIG

The decision was made. We were quitting our jobs, putting our lives on hold, and hitting the road to fulfill a dream. We set a date—April 15—hoping to leave before the Louisiana summer heat set in. There was only one thing standing in our way: we didn't have a van.

We started the quest for our future home-on-wheels where any good search starts nowadays: online. Dustin spent a lot of time searching for "the one," the rig that would be our home, that would navigate all the national parks and backroads, shelter us from storms, give us shade from the sun. At the time, there wasn't much online about vanlife, as the movement was in its infancy. There were no hundred-thousand-dollar, tricked-out Mercedes Sprinters to drool over, no campervan rental companies offering a "try before you buy" vanlife experience. We were starting from scratch, a blank canvas.

Researching the term "campervan" online turned up a small variety of inhabitable vehicle options, from RVs to truck campers. We combed through page after page of Google image results trying to find something that fit the vision we had in our minds. There were cargo vans with mattresses thrown in the back, converted minivans with storage and a bed, those little pop-up campers you can pull with your car. But the one that stood out in our minds and showed up on every page in the search results was the classic, iconic Volkswagen Bus.

At the time we didn't know #vanlife existed. But we did know about the hippie movement of the sixties and the vehicle that embodied it. The VW Bus is a symbol of counterculture, of love and empathy, of untethered freedom. And each one we came across was a bright and beautiful color. Neither Dustin nor I had ever seen one up close, much less been inside one, so we scoured the internet for details. When we learned they came equipped with a bed and a tiny kitchen, we were floored. *It has everything we need*, I thought. But that was my inexperience talking. Truth is, I had no idea what we'd need, nor what obstacles we'd face living in a van on the road. For days we discussed our options, but I couldn't get the image of the colorful VW Bus out of my mind. I could picture Dustin in the driver's seat cruising down the highway with me riding shotgun, feet on the dash, waving at everyone we drove past. Based on that image, we finally agreed, the VW Bus was the one for us.

Now all we had to do was find the right one for sale. This proved much more difficult than I had imagined. A lack of air-conditioning meant the bus was far from the ideal vehicle for the balmy South, and nearly all the ones that we found for sale lived out west. Most were in California, with the closest ones residing in Colorado. It was early March at this point, and Dustin and I were about to celebrate two years of marriage. A weekend getaway to clear our heads and contemplate this major life decision seemed exactly like the thing we needed. And, we figured, why not take this opportunity to scout out our future home-on-wheels?

I found a quaint little cabin in the mountains of Colorado and booked our flights while Dustin arranged for us to test-drive some Volkswagens. We picked up our rental car in Denver and drove straight to the first owner's house. There it was, a green-and-yellow bus. It was cute, but to my surprise, it was smaller than I'd thought. "They look so much bigger online," I whispered to Dustin. We took it for a spin, and I felt good sitting in the front seat, but it was noisy on the highway and not at all cozy. The low ceiling meant we'd have to crouch down inside; plus its top speed was only about fifty-five miles per hour.

The second one was a beautiful lime green with a brand-new engine. This one had a pop top. The beautiful canopy opened up to an expansive headspace and a second bed. It ran much better than the first, getting all the way up to sixty miles per hour. While Dustin tried to negotiate the price with the owner, I attempted to get a feel for the living space, with its cute little couch that pulled out into a bed, a table on a swivel, and a tiny sink and stove. While functional, it was still too small and the interior was old and cracked. I just couldn't see myself making this van a home.

We spent the weekend in the cabin trying to enjoy our romantic getaway, but I couldn't help feeling nervous that we were still so far away from finding a rig. Flying back to New Orleans empty-handed had us both feeling stressed and, by now, a little desperate. We started weighing the pros and cons of flying out to California, where there was an abundance of options, and hunting for our new home-on-wheels. I would stay in New Orleans and

finish packing while Dustin searched. As much as we both despised the idea, we felt like there was no other choice. Pickings were slim and desperate times called for desperate measures.

A couple of weeks after returning from Colorado, Dustin called me frantically into the kitchen: "Come check this out." I ran in and he turned his laptop screen toward me, and there it was: a Volkswagen Vanagon. It was the first time I had seen one, bigger and more modern than the bus, with a pop top, and this one even had its own website. The exciting news that had Dustin all flustered was that it was in our own backyard in Mobile, Alabama, only two hours away. With both of us close to bursting with excitement and anxiety, Dustin set up an appointment to see it the next day, two weeks from the date we were set to leave New Orleans.

MEETING WALDEN

We were biting our nails as we drove from New Orleans to Mobile. Dustin had done the research on the van we were looking at and it sounded perfect, almost too good to be true. The website detailed everything about it, every mechanical job that was done and every addition made. It seemed like a real beauty.

It was owned by a professor who had just moved to Mobile from the Bay Area. The van was a family heirloom, passed down to him from his father. He had recently lived in it for six months on a cross-country road trip, documenting the journey on his blog, which had garnered a dedicated following. In reading through his blog, you could really tell that he loved his van. This gave me hope that it was well cared for.

As we rounded the corner toward the professor's house, I spotted it, a tan beauty with a bright blue canopy sitting proudly in the driveway, nose pointing toward the road, as if to say, *I'm ready for my next adventure.* "The paint looks good," I said as we pulled up and parked. We were feeling both excitement and fear. Deep down, I already knew this was the one.

On the front of the roof there was a sticker with the name Walden. *And it has a name,* I thought. We walked up the driveway and Dustin went to the door. I walked around the van inspecting it as best I knew how. "No prominent rust spots," I said quietly. This was one of the things we learned to look for since seeing the last two Westys. These old vans are prone to rust, which is expensive to treat and, if left unchecked, can deteriorate the body of the van. Dustin and I made a pact before we went—if it's mechanically sound, has no major rust, and the owner will meet us at our budget, we'd get it. So far, so good.

We spent the next five hours chatting with the owner and learning the ins and outs of this van. He walked us through the engine—well, truth be told, he explained this mostly to Dustin, since that's more of his expertise than mine. While this was happening, I pulled out the loft bed, lay inside, and imagined this being my new home. It was cozy and had a cute little built-in kitchen. The van came with numerous amenities that hadn't even crossed my mind as being useful: a marine fridge, a solar panel, and a propane

furnace. I dreamt of all the adventures we'd have together, all the meals I would cook, all the new friends I would entertain. What I could not have imagined was how much this van would change my life, how much growth I would make in it, how much it would teach me.

I napped briefly and was awakened by the engine starting. "Want to take it for a spin?" said the owner. We headed straight for the interstate and got it up to speed, a respectable sixty-five miles per hour. After half an hour alone, we decided this was the one, and we were ready to take our van home.

But we had to get out of the driveway first. It was dark by that time, and we still had a two-hour drive ahead of us. So, after writing the biggest check we had ever jointly written, Dustin attempted to leave the driveway with me following behind in my car. The van started right up but there was no movement. I waited for a while and finally got out of my car and walked over.

"What's wrong? I'm ready to go."

"The headlights won't come on." Dustin walked up to the porch and knocked on the door. The previous owner answered in his pajamas and Dustin explained the situation. He went back into the house, soon returned with a bag of tools, handed them to Dustin, and said, "Good luck," then shut the door. The message was clear: the van was ours now, and this was our first challenge.

Dustin pulled the fuse panel down from behind the dash. He checked every fuse, traced every wire, tweaked and screwed and tested everything, but nothing worked. The mosquitos came out and bit us as we toiled, me shining a flashlight and silently hoping, Dustin tooling around in Walden's innards. *This is our initiation,* I thought. The mosquitos, the dark, our hungry bellies, being left out alone with no one to help—would we get past this, or would we fail?

After more than an hour of stress and worry, we were on the road and on our way back to New Orleans with our new van home. To this day, we have no idea what was wrong that night, or how Dustin fixed it. Or maybe it fixed itself—Vanagons do that sometimes. Little did we know that this would be the first of many breakdowns that would test our will to keep going.

IRIE

Walden was a popular van by the time we found him, with a dedicated fanbase thanks to his previous owner's travel blog. Though we loved the story of Walden, we knew we were writing our own story and needed to give it a name that aligned with our journey. We didn't immediately know what that would be, but we knew innately that she wasn't a Walden.

We wanted something fun, something we could grow with, and, most important, something that reflected our feelings and our journey. Ruminating on my Caribbean roots led me to the name Irie.

Irie [I-rie/I '-ree], noun. Powerful and pleasing; the state of feeling great.

There was so much to this name that is meaningful to me. Growing up in Trinidad, I heard this word all the time and it's a part of my culture.

Irie is a patois word used in the Caribbean as a friendly greeting to describe feeling good; everything is all right. The word *Irie* has deep spiritual meaning in the Rastafari culture, signifying a state of peace. And on this new journey, we were seeking Irie; the ultimate, all-encompassing positive experience. Our van was now Irie, the tan Vanagon with a bright blue canopy.

We spent two weeks after purchasing Irie working tirelessly to get her fine-tuned and ready for life on the road. This was when we both ac-

cepted that Dustin would be our in-house mechanic. He spent most of our last weeks in New Orleans lying on the street in front of our apartment underneath Irie, looking at her innards and talking quietly to himself.

I don't think we said much to each other those last few days, as we had both succumbed to all the emotions of change—anxiety, fear, excitement. I held two big yard sales and filled my time downsizing, sorting, and selling off our personal belongings to make extra cash in preparation for the financial uncertainty. When I wasn't doing that, I was trying to figure out how to fit what was left of our life into eighty square feet.

We set out on the road with Irie in the spring of 2016 (nearly seven years ago at the time of this writing). And we've been roaming America's open roads in this old tin can ever since. In 2019 we took on a new riding partner, our eighty-pound lap dog Amara the German Shepherd. We've crisscrossed the country and traveled up and down the West Coast more times than we can count, but we still find new places to explore. New Orleans is and always will be our "home base." And when the air turns crisp, it's a reminder for us snowbirds to escape the wrath of winter and head south, usually to Baja, Mexico.

Vanlife was never in my initial plan. In fact, when we made the decision to move into a van, we didn't know the term #vanlife was a thing. We just knew we wanted to explore the open roads and national parks of America the Beautiful. We gave ourselves one year to try out this lifestyle: New Orleans to Alaska to see the aurora borealis, then back again.

But as you'll see in the pages that follow, we quickly learned that nothing ever works out the way you imagine. And when you live in a classic old rig like ours, you'd better believe you'll never make it to where you're going without a breakdown adventure. Through it all, the past years have prepared me for however long this journey will take me. Maybe we'll finally make it to everywhere on our wish list. And with all the upgrades we've made to our Irie, maybe we'll have one summer without a breakdown—though, probably not.

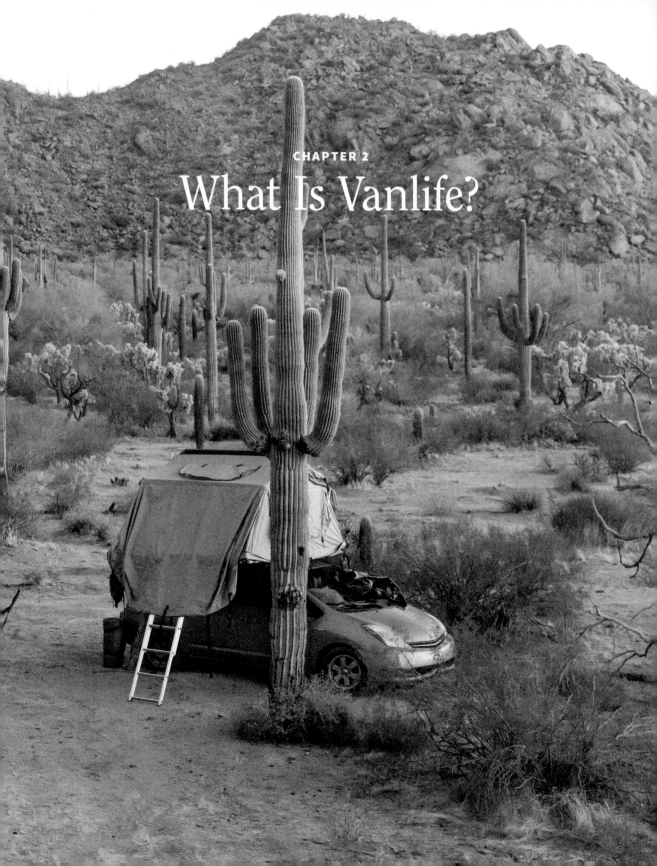

CHAPTER 2
What Is Vanlife?

Vanlife [van-līf], noun.

Simply put, vanlife is the act of dwelling in a van, either full-time or part-time. However, in recent years "vanlife" has become an umbrella term referring to dwelling in any vehicle, including RVs, skoolies, cars, truck campers, and more. These rigs/vessels are often converted to include basic comforts: a bed, stove, sink, fridge, solar panels, running water, and even toilets and showers. But all these amenities are certainly not necessary to live vanlife.

I've had the opportunity to connect with vanlifers from all over the world: online through social media, in-person at gatherings and events, and in beautiful chance encounters on the road. One thing we all have in common is the desire to take control of our lives. Whether seeking adventure, financial independence, a life of simplicity and minimalism, or a break from the rat race, for those of us with the privilege to choose this lifestyle, vanlife provides the opportunity to live a life that is in harmony with one's own ideals and values.

Once an under-the-radar lifestyle, #vanlife has evolved into a global social movement since the early 2010s, and has only grown in popularity. In this book, we'll focus primarily on vanlife as it relates to the North American road traveler.

An individual who chooses this lifestyle is referred to as a "vanlifer," but it's important to note that not everyone lives this way by choice or identifies with this moniker. Vanlifers come in all shapes and sizes, races, genders, and socioeconomic backgrounds. And "vans," as I just mentioned, can range from a Prius with a pop-up rooftop tent, to a tricked-out Mercedes Sprinter, and everything in between. But for many vanlifers, their vehicle isn't the central component, just as a runner isn't defined by the shoes they wear. For us, the van is merely a tool, whereas "vanlife" is a way of life.

THE HIPPIE MOVEMENT

Vandwelling or van culture, as we know it, is not a new concept. It has always been at the heart

The act of living in a van; vandwelling.

of counterculture. The hippie movement of the sixties essentially created a free-spirited sub-culture, one that was influential to the modern vanlife movement. While the word "hippie" tends to make some people cringe, to many it's a term of endearment as its existence is a direct result of many major social and political struggles. As a movement, it had a significant impact on society and served to shape the ideals and values of many individuals.

Most hippies of the sixties were likely not seeking to inspire a movement. Rather, they were individuals disillusioned by the ideals and practices of American society and the picture-perfect image of their parents' generation. Just like many modern vanlifers, they were searching for a more liberated lifestyle.

The symbol of this free-spirited movement was, and still is, the iconic Volkswagen Bus. And while it may not have been the first vehicle of vanlife, the VW Bus was certainly the most well-known and most influential. It's the epitome of

unconventionality, serving as an emblem of the counterculture revolution, an embodiment of the quest for untethered freedom, a bona fide symbol of protest.

As the hippie movement fizzled out, the ideals that it stood for lived on in the image of these classic old vans. They evolved to represent a form of escapism, where modern-day nomads could pursue a life outside of societal norms. The VW bus served as a symbol of hope then, and it still does today.

Dustin and I are not immune to this nostalgia. And though our Irie is the younger sibling of the "hippie bus," the sentimentality is still present. We experience it in the faces of children whose jaws drop as we drive past; in the outstretched hand of a fellow motorist held high out the window, two fingers proudly flashing a peace sign; in the glimmering eyes of old-timers who hold us hostage at gas pumps to regale us with tales of days past, recalling their own pursuit of a life of peace and love in a VW van.

I'd be remiss if I didn't mention one of the major precursors that paved the way for someone like me to have the ability to live a life of road travel in America: *The Negro Motorist Green Book*.

The Negro Motorist Green Book, best known as the *Green Book*, was started in 1936 by Harlem postman Victor Hugo Green. This guide was published over three decades and was an indispensable resource that helped African Americans travel the country safely and with dignity, during a time of Jim Crow laws and segregation when Black travelers faced threats of racist violence, including lynching.*

The *Green Book* listed towns, restaurants, motels, gas stations, and other stops across the country where Black motorists were welcome and safe. And it played a critical role in expanding opportunities for Black travelers by helping them find not only essentials but also entertainment, leisure, and community on the road. The *Green Book* is a part of American history that revolutionized the Black experience in road travel.

There will be a day sometime in the near future when this guide will not have to be published. That is when we as a race will have equal opportunities and privileges in the United States. It will be a great day for us to suspend this publication for then we can go wherever we please, and without embarrassment.

—Victor Hugo Green

* See https://negromotoristgreenbook.si.edu/about/.

#VANLIFE AS A SOCIAL, MODERN MOVEMENT

In more modern times, the culture has shifted, with emphasis placed on aesthetic appeal and modern comforts. Some campervans are luxurious, almost mini rolling apartments. If you have the cash and are willing to invest, you can convert virtually any vehicle into a comfortable abode with all the conveniences of a stationary home.

At the same time, #vanlife has become synonymous with "Insta-worthy" photos and artistically built campervans that are unattainable for many. This romanticized vision is harmful and has created a false narrative and a perceived barrier to entry for numerous people. So before we go too far, I'm here to say that you don't need a decked-out rig to live this lifestyle. In fact, nearly anyone with a vehicle can live vanlife. This level of accessibility is a key reason why vanlife is one of the most sought-after lifestyles of today.

Like any subset of society, vanlife culture has a variety of different participants and carries meaning far beyond style and aesthetic appeal. For me, it has been a means toward a more intentional life and realigning with my core values, tapping into my passions, and reigniting my relationship with nature. For many outside the glamorized version portrayed on social media, vanlife is simply a necessity.

Vanlifers engage in this lifestyle for many reasons. For one, it's an existence that fosters diverse communities. Whether you're an older hippie living through the sentiments of the sixties, a digital nomad finding inspiration on the open road, a trust-fund baby, a wayward millennial, or something else entirely, there is space for everyone in vanlife.

Today vanlife has new relevance. Thanks to the internet, "work" doesn't have to take place in the office. Over the years, our Irie has evolved from a basic campervan to a fully equipped rolling office studio. While it's taken a lot of trial and error to figure out exactly what we need to create an off-grid digital nomad life, over time we've managed to put all the pieces together. As the movement has grown, so has the demand for technology that makes this way of life possible. And remote jobs are becoming more common than ever, especially since the COVID-19 pandemic.

Vanlife, alongside modern technology, has spawned a new niche—overland digital nomadism—which has played a large role in the explosion of the modern vanlife movement. Practically any job that relies on a computer can be executed remotely. That encompasses endless career possibilities. Many vanlife digital nomads are artists, photographers, videographers, graphic designers, writers, and content creators, but there are new professions that are constantly being added to that mix.

This divergence from the typical office-work arrangement continues to inspire people to live more nomadically, making it possible for virtually anyone with a computer to sustain a roaming lifestyle. In this way, modern-day nomads are challenging the status quo by reimagining work and careers and blazing new paths to success and happiness.

It's no secret that modern technology, cool gadgets, fancy gear, high-end van builds, and the ability to work from anywhere have made vanlife more appealing to the masses. But for us, and for many vanlifers, the main purpose of this lifestyle remains, in essence, a way to take control of our existence and shift away from a consumer-driven way of living.

The vanlife movement has grown exponentially since Dustin and I hit the road in 2016. We've borne witness to the rise of diverse, niche communities that are shaping and strengthening its makeup. In the late summer of 2019, I founded Diversify Vanlife, a social media platform turned community organization, in response to the lack of representation of BIPOC and other marginalized people within the vanlife community. Since then, Diversify Vanlife has become a movement in its own right.

It's the people of vanlife and our drive to challenge the status quo, to reclaim our freedom, to take up space, to shift the narrative and choose our own paths, to dismantle systems put in place to marginalize us—that's what makes the vanlife movement so impactful. We are redefining community, and community is the heartbeat of the vanlife movement, which I speak directly to in a later chapter.

HOW DO YOU VANLIFE?

One of the biggest misconceptions of vanlife is that you have to quit your job, sell all your belongings, and uproot your entire life to live in a van. Granted, that's how Dustin and I got started, but I don't recommend it, unless you're a head-first-into-things kind of person, like me.

So how do you actually "live the vanlife"? There are many ways, as varied as the types of individuals who live this lifestyle. The great thing is, you don't have to commit to full-time vanlife to enjoy the perks.

TYPES OF VANLIFERS

For our purposes, there are three main classifications of vanlifer: full-time, part-time, and weekender.

Full-time Vanlifer: A "full-timer" is anyone whose vehicle serves as their primary, year-round residence. Dustin and I are full-time traveling vanlifers, though not all full-time vanlifers travel. There are many people who live in their rig in a stationary location.

Part-time Vanlifer: "Part-timers" maintain roots in a stationary location, typically having a permanent or stationary home, and spend several weeks, months, or full seasons living and traveling in their rig.

Weekender: This is the broadest category of all. Weekend warriors live in their primary, stationary residence for reasons such as work, school, or family commitments. They take advantage of weekends, holidays, and vacations to travel and adventure. Of course, some people work on weekends and adventure during the week. We call these folks "savvy weekenders."

Before living vanlife full-time, Dustin and I were weekend warriors. We'd stack up PTO, take advantage of every long weekend, load up my sedan, and drive eight hours to the mountains of northern Georgia, just so we could scratch our wanderlust itch. It was a taste of the freedom of road travel.

VANLIFE VESSELS

Although the term "vanlife" implies living in a van, there are many types of vehicles that can be converted to livable homes-on-wheels. These conversions can be elaborate or simple and can be designed around your needs, vanlife type, and budget.

> **Here are some of the most popular candidates for alternative rolling home conversions:**
>
> - Volkswagen Vanagon or Bus (like our Irie)
> - Dodge Ram ProMaster
> - Ford Transit and Econoline
> - Mercedes Sprinter
> - SUV
> - station wagon
> - school bus (skoolie)
> - shuttle bus
> - box truck/retired delivery van
> - military van
> - converted ambulance or hearse
> - pickup truck camper
> - travel trailer
> - RV
> - cargo van
> - minivan

NUANCES OF VANLIFE (VANLIFE PERSONAS)

Another misconception is that people living in vans spend most of their time driving or camping in nature, but there are many nuances to this lifestyle that get left behind in the mainstream conversation. As I've noted, vanlife is a spectrum, and the types of vanlifers are as varied as the rigs they inhabit. Keep in mind, these aren't hard-and-fast definitions but rather terms I've provided to illustrate a few of the nuances of the vanlife experience. Over the span of our vanlife journey, Dustin and I have fallen into, out of, and overlapped most of these loose categories at various times.

The Slow Traveler: Stays in one place for weeks at a time. They use their van as a home base for exploring or as a temporary campsite office. Many eco-conscious vanlifers tend to adopt a slower approach to road travel.

The Adventure Junkie: Climbers, surfers, powder chasers. The minimal overhead associated with vanlife allows these travelers to spend most of their time adventuring and less time chasing the almighty dollar. They typically go wherever the action is, moving with the seasons.

The Aspiring Entrepreneur: Low overhead means less time working for a paycheck and more time working on passion projects. The wealth of time this lifestyle provides, coupled with a diversity of perspectives, is a ripe situation for an aspiring entrepreneur.

The Seeker: May or may not fall into any of the other categories. These vandwellers, unfulfilled by traditional life trajectories, are searching for inspiration, direction, and freedom. Whether they are a young adult fresh out of school, an individual going through a career change or mid- or early-life crisis, or a retiree—this could be a person of any age or background, but one thing they all have in common is that they approach this lifestyle with an open mind and an open heart.

The Nature Lover: Long to wake up each day surrounded by trees and birds rather than houses and cars? A mobile off-grid home means you can go as far as you like and stay for as long as you want. These outdoorists travel for the purpose of being immersed in the natural world.

The "See and Do It All"-er: Moves quickly, rarely staying in one place for more than a few days. They're always looking for a new place to explore and a new state to check off the list.

The Frugal Professional: Full-time job, financially savvy, works for a company based in the city and can afford to pay rent on an apartment or house but chooses vanlife to save money, invest more capital, and/or pay off debt.

These shrewd nonconformists challenge the status quo in their own way as they merge the goal-oriented drive of capitalist society with the de-commodified minimalism of vanlife.

The Houseless: Living in a vehicle means not living on the street. Vandwelling can be a viable, safe option for many individuals who face housing instability, financial misfortune, poverty, violence, disability, or mental illness.

Tethered by proximity to the city for family, community, employment, and/or resources, these individuals live vanlife out of necessity.

The Stationary Vanlifer: Have van, will (not) travel. Busting the stigma of "living in a van down by the river," these full-timers enjoy the benefits of this unconventional lifestyle with the comforts and convenience of staying in a fixed location.

THE MOLEHILL MINDSET

Have you heard the expression "making a mountain out of a molehill"? I believe that the molehill mindset is why many of us never go after our deepest desires. And for some, depending on demographic—nationality, racial and ethnic background, social identity—there are expectations so ingrained that they can prohibit us from realizing our dreams. As a first-generation immigrant, the pressure to live up to familial expectations of being the one who "made it" almost kept me from seeing the possibility of taking control of my life's trajectory. Even though my family lived abroad, I was still terrified of what they would think of me and how they would feel about my new lifestyle if people in my village were to find out. This brought on a lot of shame and guilt, which exacerbated the fear of disappointing my loved ones.

The molehill mindset tells us that the challenge is insurmountable, that it's going to be too hard to overcome, so we never get started. Don't get me wrong—the decision to go against the predefined road map that society has laid out for us is big, but not big enough to stop us from pursuing our own path.

Here are a few questions to ask yourself if you're considering vanlife.

- What are my top three reasons for considering vanlife?
- Do I want to travel, and if so, how much?
- Do I want to live vanlife full-time, part-time, or travel on weekends?
- If full-time, for how long?
- Can I try out vanlife part-time in my current rig? (Remember, you don't need a van to experience vanlife.)
- How will I sustain myself financially?
- Will I travel solo or with a partner?
- What are my most important needs?
- What are some conveniences I can't live without?
- Am I willing to sell my belongings, or do I want to put them in storage?
- What kind of van suits my needs?
- Am I comfortable leaving my stationary community/family/friends?

Ask yourself this question: To what in my life am I giving more power than it deserves? Whatever it may be, I can pretty much guarantee it more closely resembles a molehill than a mountain. Next time you notice these feelings filling back up and becoming a negative force in your day-to-day life, ask yourself, "Are these feelings helping me?" Usually the answer is no.

Without a doubt, the uncertainty and unpredictability of this lifestyle remain real and tangible. But with more and more people from all walks of life embracing it, the barriers to entry, stigmas, and fears about its viability that have made it unattainable for many are being challenged, lowered, removed, and squashed.

For BIPOC inspired to embark on your own vanlife journey, here are some things to consider if you're facing challenges stemming from cultural expectations.

Put it into perspective:
○ What are the expectations that are presenting challenges?
○ Are they my own or someone else's?
○ Do these expectations reflect what I want for my life?
○ Are they creating limiting beliefs for me?
○ Are they still relevant to the world today?

It's okay to reimagine a new path for yourself. Take time to cultivate your inner voice and clarify your desires. Stepping away from the noise helps to put things into perspective—journal, talk to like-minded and supportive people in your life. The BIPOC road travel community has grown significantly in recent years, so you're not alone.

CHAPTER 3

Pros & Cons of Vanlife

You've seen it on social media—
the well-curated photos of
beautiful people in their decked-out,
custom-built rigs, lounging
in picturesque landscapes with
stunning backdrops.

They grab your attention and pull you into a dreamy world on the other side of the screen, where the vans are always neat and tidy, and the people are well-groomed, shiny, and showered.

I love those photos, and constantly find myself gobbling them up as I scroll through my feed. They're inspiring and trigger feelings of freedom and wonder, and at times can serve as a means of escape for many of us. While these picture-perfect images may be real for some, for most of us out here on the open road every day, the reality of vanlife is often messy and challenging. In the Irie van, it shows up as dirt, sweat, and tears from frequent breakdowns, inclement weather, cluttered space, quarrels, weeks gone without a shower, too-hot days followed by too-cold nights, sleeping in parking lots and peeing in bottles, getting covered in dust and dog hair, and always having dirty feet. But that's the thing about vanlife, it's often a beautiful mess. Although the cons can be discouraging, when you get those

awe-inspiring landscapes and crisp, starry nights around the campfire, the challenging times are redeemed. At the end of the day, dear friend, it's all worth it to me.

My many years on the road continue to be a teacher, gifting lessons and stories that I hope to someday regale my grandkids with after I've finally traded my van for a rocking chair. Until then, I share with you my catalog of top vanlife pros and cons.

PROS

1. CREATE THE LIFE YOU WANT TO LIVE

Travel has a way of putting things into perspective. Before joining the vanlife movement, I was caught up in preconceived notions of what my life should be: go to college, follow the "right path," and eventually achieve the American Dream. I was so consumed by the noise of everyone else's opinions that I subtly cut myself off from what I wanted. I was serving not my own agenda but someone else's. Living vanlife has allowed me to change that mindset.

Choosing a life of travel meant stepping away from society's norms. For me, living in a van brought me closer to nature where external distractions tend to fade away. Vanlife has been the catalyst through which I have found the space to sit quietly and tune into myself. I've taken the time to reevaluate my life's trajectory, to step out of my comfort zone, to experiment, and to try new things.

The photography included in these pages is just one example of the liberation that vanlife has brought me. I've always had a passion for this art, but before vanlife, it was a distant dream. On the road, I've created space to be led by the calling. Now I'm proud to say I'm a photographer.

Pro Tip: Travel slowly. It's easy to get caught up wanting to see and do it all, but magic happens when you travel at the speed of slow. It allows you to develop a real sense of place and create space to cultivate personal growth.

2. YOUR HOME IS ALWAYS WITH YOU

On Memorial Day weekend in 2019, Dustin and I went off-grid to explore the beautiful terrain surrounding Goblin Valley State Park in Utah. By the time we arrived, the sun was low on the horizon and the rugged trek to find a dispersed campsite had us maneuvering in the dark. We finally found the perfect place to camp, but as soon as we pulled off the road we were stuck, back tires spinning out of control. It was late, we were tired and hungry, and tempers were beginning to flare. Recognizing that we needed to admit defeat in that moment, Dustin jacked up the van to level, we popped the top, opened a bag of potato chips, watched a movie, and went to bed.

Vanlife throws a lot of unforeseen circumstances your way, but one constant is that your home is always with you.

Pro Tip: Keep a vanlife arsenal of tools and recovery gear. Murphy's Law says anything that can go wrong will, and this is certainly true for vanlife. Be prepared by always having a set of basic mechanic tools, jumper cables, tow strap, and a good jack. These are essential components of any vanlife arsenal.

3. SUSTAINABLE, OFF-GRID LIVING

There's a misconception that living in a van and traveling means having a big carbon footprint. But that's not always the case. When we lived in New Orleans, Dustin and I drove two cars. We both commuted an hour each way, which means four hours' worth of fossil fuel pollution. When we got home, we heated and cooled a 1,500-square-foot apartment.

Digital nomadism has replaced all our previous outputs. Our home and office now encompass approximately eighty square feet, which is completely powered by solar energy. This mostly self-sustaining setup gives us the ability to go anywhere we choose and stay as long as we want. For me, this untethered freedom is the embodiment of vanlife.

Pro Tip: Invest in solar power. In recent years, the demand for and availability of solar components has exploded. Now, getting a plug-and-play solar kit for your rig is more affordable than ever. Renewable energy, combined with slow travel as mentioned above, can not only save you money but also reduce your fossil fuel footprint.

4. THE ABILITY TO LEAVE

In 2016, Dustin and I had this wild idea to spend a snowy winter in the van. We planned to go skiing and snowshoeing and enjoy a winter wonderland outdoors in the Pacific Northwest. But our plans were derailed when a major breakdown left us stranded in the mountains of Oregon. After a miserable week lying on the frozen earth rebuilding Irie's engine, we were exhausted, cold, and each questioning our life decisions. It was the lowest of lows. But after bringing Irie back to life, we packed up the van and headed south, all the way to Baja, Mexico, for some much-needed warmth and space to contemplate our next steps.

In this lifestyle, there will always be detours and bumps in the road (literally and figuratively). But during that frigid winter, we learned that we can be as flexible as we want and change like the wind. This ability to leave when things aren't working is a power almost no other lifestyle can offer.

Pro Tip: Be flexible. Vanlife teaches us many lessons, perhaps none more important than learning to let go and be flexible. Our plans may get us where we want to go, but flexibility takes us where we need to be.

5. LOW-COST LIVING

I've been officially debt-free since 2020. A lower cost of living, less overhead, and less pressure to consume have made this possible. Since hitting the road, Dustin and I have gone through it all financially speaking; from broke, pinching pennies, and sitting still because we didn't have gas money, to living more comfortably as our income has increased. This is definitely a perk of vanlife: it can be done with a tight budget or deep pockets. The reality is that most people live this way on a budget, even though it might seem otherwise on Instagram.

Thanks to the low cost of living, I've been able to say yes to opportunities and take on passion projects that offered little to no financial compensation at first. This has opened doors to new and exciting opportunities that otherwise would not have been possible if I had other expenses to worry about.

Pro Tip: Eliminate unnecessary expenses. Vanlife can be the vehicle for saving money, freeing up time, and even finding financial independence. Maximize your opportunities by minimizing or eliminating any unnecessary bills and expenses before you get on the road.

6. REDEFINE COMMUNITY

I celebrated six months on the road at my first van gathering in Bend, Oregon. Up to that point, Dustin and I hadn't met anyone who was doing what we were—leaving behind a conventional life for full-time life on the road in a van. But immersed in the forests of Oregon, surrounded by more than a hundred vans, we found community.

The experience of connecting with like-minded vanlifers empowered us to keep going. It bridged the gap of what had been missing in those lonely early months on the road—a social connection, sense of belonging, and people we could relate to. Living a life of uncertainty is a norm of vanlife, but knowing I had a support network with my new community helped me to feel a little bit safer and stave off the occasional feelings of hopelessness.

There's something special about the connections we make with other nomads. Maybe it's because we know we'll soon say goodbye and our paths may never again cross, but the bonds forged are deep and authentic, enduring long after we part. And with each encounter, our circle grows. Over the years we've built a diverse network of people from all backgrounds, professions, and walks of life. Through countless collaborations, we've found the means to facilitate entrepreneurship on the road. For the better, vanlife has reshaped our definitions of community, neighborhood, and success.

Pro Tip: Connect with community online. Community used to mean the people you live near or interact with on a regular basis. Thanks to modern technology, we no longer have to limit our community to our geographical location. Connect with fellow road travelers on social media and build a diverse network of individuals from all backgrounds, races, cultures, and walks of life. This creates opportunities and contributes to an inclusive community.

7. SIMPLICITY & MINIMALISM

Three months into vanlife we stopped at a Goodwill and unloaded half our possessions.

Dustin and I often joke that we're accidental minimalists. Vanlife tailored our life in that direction because it forced us to be mindful of our consumption and reevaluate our priorities. The things we now value aren't really things at all. The simplicity that we've embraced through this minimalist lifestyle has given us the space and energy we needed to live more intentionally. We've gained the tools and the ability to focus our attention on what matters most to us—our passions, ourselves, our community, and each other. One of the biggest benefits of this has been reducing financial burdens. We're no longer keeping up with the Joneses and the Kardashians of the world or living with the stress that comes from it.

Pro Tip: Embrace a minimalist way of living. Learning to live with less is a key lesson in vanlife, but you don't have to go cold turkey. Take inventory of the things in your life and begin reducing what you don't need or use regularly. Keep in mind, minimalism is about what you value, and there is no right or wrong way to do it.

8. FREEDOM TO CHOOSE

In 2016, I chose to reevaluate my life's trajectory. This was one of the scariest things I've ever done. But I follow the mantra "If you're not asking yourself *What the hell am I doing with my life?* you're not doing it right." Since that warm spring day with New Orleans in the rearview mirror, I've been asking myself that question. It certainly hasn't been easy. I work more now than I ever have, but the difference is, it's all my choice. I love my work and I love that I get to decide how I want to live and what experiences I want to have. Entrepreneurship was always something I desired, and in this untethered lifestyle, I'm able to choose how I get there.

Pro Tip: Prioritize your passions as soon as possible. This will allow you to find the things you truly enjoy and focus your time on developing your skills in ways that will benefit you personally and professionally. Turning a hobby into a business is a real possibility on the road.

CONS

1. LIMITED RESOURCES

I can't count how many times the tap has run dry mid-shower, or the propane has run out with a pot of pasta halfway boiled on the stove. This leaves us packing up camp and heading into town, and that's no fun when you've got a head full of shampoo. When you have to harvest your own electricity and find places to fill water and propane, you learn to appreciate them. You become more intentional with how you use these precious resources. This is a learning curve for many, considering the American culture of abundance and overconsumption.

I've learned that keeping things simple is the best way to conserve resources. One-pot meals have become my go-to, as it conserves fuel and saves water by minimizing dirty dishes. And I ain't got no shame about eating out of the pot either. Charging devices during the day allows us to use power as it's being produced (free solar energy, woohoo!) rather than using the power stored in the battery. This saves our battery power for the things that still need to run at night, like the refrigerator.

Pro Tip: Adopt habits to help conserve resources. Water, power, and fuel are the three most essential and limited resources in vanlife.

2. FINANCIAL UNCERTAINTY

For me, opting for a life on the road meant leaving behind the security of a nine-to-five job with a steady paycheck, health insurance, and 401(k). In my first year of vanlife, I was fully dependent on my partner's income. Fortunately, Dustin was able to parlay his job into a part-time remote position that allowed us to keep gas in the tank and food in the fridge. While I was grateful, this was the first time in my adult life I was financially dependent on anyone, which caused me a great deal of stress and anxiety. It felt like I was doubling down on the uncertainties, stepping into a new life while severing the ties that had brought me a sense of self-worth and independence.

The financial uncertainty associated with life on the road can be the biggest obstacle for anyone considering vanlife. Fortunately, remote work has become much more common since the onset of COVID-19. And in our digital age, it's easier than ever before to become a digital nomad. I'll go into more detail on how to make money on the road in a later chapter.

Pro Tip: Seek out freelance gigs or remote work before you hit the road. Money may not be the primary motivator for many vanlifers, but unfortunately it's something we can't live without. If possible, parlay your current job into a remote position. Read Chapter 9: How to Make Money on the Road.

3. SPACE IS AT A PREMIUM

As I've noted, I'm an accidental minimalist. Living in eighty square feet forced me to choose what possessions were most valuable to me. Though it didn't come easy. When we first moved into the van, I brought along most of my wardrobe plus the kitchen sink. Two large storage containers of clothes occupied the space behind our bench seat. Every evening we'd shuffle things from the bottom bunk to the loft before we could get to bed. This was exhausting, especially since I wore the same three outfits over and over. A few months in, I made a large donation to Goodwill.

But storage is just one part of spatial constraints. When you're cohabiting in a tiny space, every movement becomes a dance. Early on, Dustin and I frequently stepped on each other's toes as we learned how to lead and how to follow. Over the years our ugly dance has evolved into a ballet, as we seamlessly glide around each other in our daily motions.

Pro Tip: Downsize often. Every three months, Dustin and I take inventory of our possessions in the van, and we "purge," donating our unneeded items. And to keep things light, we cycle through seasonal gear by donating it at the end of the season and thrifting whatever we need along the way.

4. VULNERABILITY TO THE ELEMENTS

As I write this, it's ninety-five degrees and I'm sitting in the van swarmed with black flies. Needless to say, tempers are on edge. Life in a van does not provide much protection from the elements. We've felt the highest of highs and the lowest of lows, from a blizzard in Oregon that numbed us to the bone, to a heatwave in Death Valley that damn near melted our souls.

There's a misconception that vanlifers spend all their time cramped in a van. For my family, vanlife means spending as much time as possible outdoors in our ever-changing backyard. So how do we deal with the elements? We chase seventy-five degrees and sunny skies. This isn't always foolproof. We've experienced thunderstorms that kept us confined to the van for days, with winds rocking us violently from side to side throughout the night. But the beauty of living a life of travel is we always have the option to leave.

Pro Tip: Keep up with weather forecasts and be intentional with your seasonal destinations. When it rains, it pours. And when you live in a van, inclement weather can be dangerous.

5. BREAKDOWNS

Van breakdowns are inevitable (cue Tom Petty). We've had more breakdowns than we can count. The most memorable was our first major one, eight months into vanlife during a blizzard in the Cascade-Siskiyou National Monument in Oregon on Christmas Day. The temperature had dropped to five degrees below zero overnight and froze the coolant in our lines. When we tried to leave the next morning, we were stopped by what sounded like an explosion, followed by smoke billowing from the engine. Just to give you an idea of how cold it really was, all our drinking water was frozen and our apples could be used as hockey pucks. The icy mountain roads made it impossible for a tow truck to reach us. So we spent the next week shivering under a kind stranger's carport with nothing but a small fire pit to thaw out our fingers and toes. I watched YouTube videos and read the Volkswagen repair manual aloud as Dustin lay on the frozen earth disassembling the engine to replace the head gasket.

I crossed my fingers as Dustin fired up the engine after putting it all back together. Hearing the van rumble to life was the sweetest sound we'd ever heard. And that's when we learned for certain that in vanlife, you'll be pushed out of your comfort zone, forced to be resourceful, learn skills you never imagined, and if you're with a partner it can be the ultimate bonding experience. Plus, when you have a breakdown, you're already home.

Pro Tip: Learn basic mechanic skills. It's not a matter of if but when, and, more often than not, it's just a little thing that leaves you stranded on the highway. Have a roadside assistance membership for when it's a big fix and you need a tow.

6. STIGMAS, STEREOTYPES & MISCONCEPTIONS

I'm a Black, mixed-race woman and I live in a van, which means I've been busting stereotypes since 2016. In the US, there is the common misconception that Black people don't camp, don't like the outdoors, and don't do vanlife. These notions are dangerous because they leave Black people and other people of color vulnerable to profiling, harassment, gatekeeping, and policing (I'll get into more of this in a later chapter).

In the West, we live in a society that values consumerism, where a big house and fancy car means that you made it. So, through this lens, people tend to view a person living in their vehicle as a bum and a failure. When Dustin and I made the decision to pursue vanlife, we were rejected by some loved ones who felt like we were throwing our lives away. This is a recurring narrative. And these stigmas also permeate into the realm of local legislation. In many cities across the US, it's illegal to live or even sleep in your vehicle, which leaves people who are forced into this lifestyle more vulnerable than they already are. The way to get rid of the stigmas surrounding vanlife is to normalize it. So if it's something you

want to do, go ahead and do it, knowing there are other people out here doing the same.

Pro Tip: Don't let the stereotypes of society stop you from pursuing the things that bring joy and happiness into your life. Keep pressing on and know you're not alone. A wise person once said, "Haters gonna hate."

7. LOSS OF ROUTINE

I'll be honest, maintaining a routine in a life of travel is nearly impossible. When I envisioned my life on the road, I pictured myself practicing yoga every morning and reading captivating fantasy novels while overlooking picturesque mountains every afternoon. I brought along all the books I had been longing to read, and not only do they take up too much space, I haven't finished one yet.

We're frequently on the go, with an ever-changing backyard. And while this is quite stimulating, not every location is conducive for laying out my yoga mat. Inclement weather and extreme temperatures also make a consistent movement routine difficult to maintain. And don't get me started on work-life balance. I feel like we're constantly in search of Wi-Fi and good cell service, which kills our flow. And when COVID-19 shuttered many coffee shops and libraries, our Wi-Fi options were drastically reduced.

Additionally, everyday tasks take longer in vanlife. The simple act of washing up and making breakfast is a chore. Without intentionality and planning, life can feel unstable. Our Irie is a transformer, meaning that every morning we convert her from a sleeping configuration to a daytime configuration. It's not ideal, but that's the reality when your bedroom is also your living room, kitchen, and office. Therefore, when we find a location that ticks all the boxes—beautiful setting, nice weather, good cell service, and level ground—we stay awhile, spread out, and resurrect some remnants of a routine.

Though, as I've come to realize how futile it is to try to hold on to a traditional sense of routine, I have redefined what that means to me. I'll dive into this more in Chapter 8.

Pro Tip: Adapt tools for self-care and mental health that can be done anywhere, like journaling, yoga, and meditation. Hanging on to a routine on the road is like trying to hold water in a fishing net. But these practices will help you when the going gets rough.

8. CLEANLINESS & HYGIENE

Vanlife is a dirty lifestyle—there's no getting around it. Even if you have a shower in your van, resources are limited. I've gone as long as two weeks without a traditional shower. It's not pleasant, but if living vanlife is your goal, the reality is you have to get used to not showering every day. My initial transition from showering once or twice a day to once or twice a week was a rude awakening. But after a few months, I got creative with how I stay clean. Bowl showers are a consistent post-workout "routine," and if water is short, I opt for a wet rag wipe down. And I've gotten used to going to bed with dirty feet. I guess that's why it's called vagabonding.

Another reality of vanlife is, unless you have

period product for me in vanlife. When I'm out in nature, I bury my blood in a cathole six to eight inches deep, and far away from water sources to prevent contamination. I then rinse my cup with a small amount of water and mild soap. If I'm in a public restroom that isn't private, I wipe my cup with toilet paper, reinsert, and wash it when I have privacy, or sometimes, I bring a bottle of water with me into the stall.

While all this may sound too gross for comfort, I can tell you firsthand that after a few weeks on the road, you start to get comfortable with your own smell, and that of your partner if you share space. Humans are adaptable, and you'll get used to it.

Pro Tip: Get creative with getting clean. Contrary to another common misconception, living in a van does not mean forgoing personal hygiene. There are many ways to get clean on the road—truck stops, gyms, rec centers, and some campgrounds and RV parks offer showers for a fee, and a solar shower bag or dip in an ice-cold river or lake is a great free way to get clean.

a toilet in your van (which I do not), you're going to be peeing on the ground and pooping in a hole. Though it usually comes with a good view, it's not particularly pleasant, especially when you have to go in the middle of the night. Public restrooms, porta-potties, and pit toilets become a luxury. And as a menstruator, I'm even more intentional with my hygiene. It's no longer as simple as going to the bathroom, emptying my menstrual cup or changing my tampon, and having free-flowing water for washing up. Out of all my available options, a menstrual cup has proven to be the best

There are a lot of different factors to consider if you're thinking of making the leap into vanlife. Ultimately, if you're willing to give up some comforts and embrace a life with less, vanlife can be an adventurous and freeing alternative to a conventional lifestyle. Living a life on the road is not always easy or fun or glamorous, but for me, the pros far outweigh the cons.

CHAPTER 4

Redefining

Minimalism

MY MINIMALIST ROOTS

I've already mentioned that Dustin and I often joke that we're accidental minimalists.

It wasn't until I was preparing to move into the van full-time that I was forced to confront my addiction to stuff.

I wasn't always this way. Growing up in Trinidad, my family lived simply. My mother and grandmother were the first low-waste, eco-conscious minimalists that I ever met, although they certainly didn't use those terms. It was merely a means of survival. At a young age, living this lifestyle instilled in me the values of hard work, frugality, and self-sufficiency. I learned to be resourceful, to sew clothes and repair broken items, to raise animals, forage, and grow food—a way of life that you may think of as homesteading. For us, it was just life.

Everything we needed, we made. Coconut coir was used for cleaning and scrubbing. Palm fronds were stripped and bound into brooms. Toothbrushes were made from small branches cut from the guava tree.

Some of my fondest memories of childhood are of times spent at my grandma's house. Her home was a small, wooden two-bedroom house on stilts. There was no plumbing or electricity, so she harvested rainwater in barrels and lit her home with oil lanterns. Around the house were animals of all kinds—chickens, ducks, goats, even a mean old donkey. Under the house, the ducks and chickens sought refuge and laid their eggs, and us grandchildren would race to collect the eggs every morning before the dogs or other animals could pilfer the nests.

Many evenings my extended family—aunts, uncles, cousins, other chosen relatives—would gather in my grandmother's yard as she cooked dinner over the fireside in a *chulha*, a traditional Indian stove made of clay and grass and fueled by dried wood. My cousins and I would run around the dirt yard playing cricket and marbles, while my uncles conspired and my aunts gossiped.

When it came time to eat, we'd all sit on the ground and share a meal of either roasted tomatoes and roti or pot bread with *aloo* or a vegetable *talkari*.

After dinner, by the warm glow of a dimly lit oil lantern in her tiny living room, Grandma would regale us with folktales and songs. One by one, each grandchild would follow her lead and seize the spotlight, entertaining the family with poetry, storytelling, dance, or music.

These were my lessons in sustainability and minimalism, born of necessity, grounded by the love of a matriarch who was determined to nurture and care for her family. As a child, this way of life seemed normal. It wasn't until I left my village and entered high school in the city that I realized my family was poor.

There, the loud confidence of city kids, boisterous in the hallways, sent my heart racing with excitement. Everyone looked fresh, dressed in crisp pressed uniforms: girls in plaid, pleated skirts with matching ties, hair slicked and groomed; boys in creased slacks, with monogrammed shirts neatly tucked in. It was obvious that aesthetics and presentation were given a lot of value. I nervously traipsed past a cluster of students flaunting fancy bookbags and name-brand sneakers. An unexpected sense of shame crept in as I lowered my eyes to my own tattered and faded shoes. As I crossed the threshold that first day of high school, I was hit with the head-spinning reality that this new world would reveal my home life as less-than.

Verbal and nonverbal cues alike served as daily reminders of my inferior status. I vividly remember being ridiculed for my threadbare clothes: "Look at she! Bush child with she batterdog shoes." The teachers did nothing to circumvent the blatantly classist subtext, openly favoring students from more affluent families. This inequity reinforced my newly internalized shame about being poor and brought with it an accompanying sense of isolation.

The delineation between the haves and the have-nots in my adolescent society was defined according to the quality of one's possessions and the social status of one's family. Living with a constant exposure to this mindset, I was led to the obvious conclusion that self-worth and success are directly tied to possessions and material excess. For the first time in my life, the way that my family lived felt wrong. This shift in perspective brought on newfound desires. The allure of city life and the yearning to break the chains of poverty and create my own destiny became my driving force. So by the time I graduated high school, I had fully bought into the idea of the American Dream and was determined to pursue it. It felt like there was no other option for me.

With that, I became the first of many things in my family: the first to leave Trinidad, the first to attend college, the first to earn a degree, the first to pursue a career and achieve financial security. With this came a sense of responsibility and a need to prove that I "made it" by acquiring all the things I had associated with success and self-worth. I immersed myself in Western consumerist society and was dazzled by it. Thus began my addiction to stuff.

REDISCOVERING MINIMALISM

I learned a while back that the "American Dream" was not meant for me. The American Dream is predicated on the notion that everyone has equal access to education and resources, and thus, equal opportunity to find success and achieve upward mobility. But that simply is not and has never been true for all Americans. For people like me, those of us who live at the intersection of marginalized identities, there are systemic roadblocks that make it impossible to achieve this idyllic benchmark of success, no matter how hard we work.

As an environmental scientist, I poured myself into my career in hopes of climbing the corporate ladder. But as a woman of color in the corporate world, the barriers I faced were insurmountable. I was left acting out a false narrative that created a deep sense of inadequacy and inner conflict within me. I filled this void with a lifestyle of overconsumption.

Yet no matter how many dresses I bought or how many drunken nights I had, satisfaction and happiness eluded me. I had been following society's road map, but I was going around in circles. The rug had been pulled out from under my feet, and I didn't know which way was up. Suddenly disillusioned, I found myself at a crossroads. Confronted by fear and ready for change, I dared to be intentional with the next steps of my life. Vanlife presented an alternative, a way to escape the noise and a chance to center my own dreams. But first I had to deal with all my physical stuff.

The act of coming face-to-face with the material possessions I had acquired throughout my fif-

teen years living in America was distressing and daunting. The most intimidating aspect by far was downsizing my three full closets. The beautiful dresses, stiletto shoes, lingerie, designer handbags, and boxes of fine jewelry that filled these spaces were items that I longed for as a teenager and, in the moment of purchasing them, they gave me a sense of self-worth and validation.

As an adult, I placed a great deal of value on my appearance and seeing these items daily was evidence of how far I had come.

Standing in my 1,500-square-foot St. Charles Avenue apartment contemplating how I would fit my life into an eighty-square-foot van exposed me to feelings of vulnerability, shame, and trepidation. It wasn't the sheer anxiety that I felt having to offload all this detritus. It was the thought of how my peers and family members would perceive me that left me grappling with the notion that I was failing. Was I choosing to be poor again? What would they all say when I told them? But even through the heart-pounding, anxious moments, I couldn't let the fear of other people's opinions shake my resolve.

REIMAGINING A LIFE WITH LESS

As I've alluded to, my adopting a minimalist lifestyle did indeed happen by accident. To be honest, I was simply trying to downsize enough so that whatever was left after moving into the van could fit into a small storage unit.

It took until the second big yard sale that we held for it to become clear: the path I was carving out for myself would be less about getting rid of things and more about embracing an intentional way of living. To see the objects that I had once placed so much value in leave in the hands of strangers was humbling. The first thing I got rid of was my beloved record player, which felt like ripping off a bandage. This wasn't the best way to start my downsizing journey—giving away something I loved and found value in—but it was my first lesson in letting go. It almost goes without saying that there was a lot of emotional work involved in the process, but it prepared me for life in a very small space and propelled me on a path that was more aligned with my truth.

Unfortunately, the homogeneity of mainstream minimalism has often fabricated a culture of exclusivity. And as the vanlife movement continues to grow in popularity, it has co-opted ideas of mainstream minimalism in a way that erroneously focuses on expensive conversions, sleek rigs with neutral tones, and monochromatic aesthetics. This false narrative sets unattainable standards for many individuals, myself included.

Throughout my vanlife journey, I've been privileged to explore different concepts of minimalism. I've welcomed those that honor my roots and empower me to not engage in things that compromise my values. The idea of redefining minimalism for myself is driven by the choice to see the world through a different lens. This has influenced many aspects of my life, including my choice to adopt low-waste living and socially conscious consumerism.

In essence, minimalism is more than just living with less, it's a shift to a more mindful and intentional way of life.

These are some key aspects of mindfulness and intentionality that I have integrated into my life. This will be unique to everyone, but I hope that you find some inspiration in my examples.

Mindfulness:

- Learning to forgive myself and extending that same forgiveness to others.
- Finding gratitude in what I have and how far I've come.
- Learning to see and appreciate the abundance in my life.
- Honoring my ancestors with the ability to choose what I want to take with me and what I want to let go of.
- Prioritizing mental and physical health and well-being. This includes going to therapy, committing to a daily movement routine, and engaging in activities that bring me joy.
- Creating the space to heal from intergenerational traumas.
- Leaning into the values that were instilled in me by my mother and grandmother.
- Practicing patience and compassion with myself and others.
- Unlearning the habit of rushing.

Intentionality:

- Removing toxicity from my life, and thus actively rejecting things, people, and situations that no longer serve me.
- Protecting my peace by being intentional about what I consume, be that news, media, or other people's opinions.
- Releasing habits that inhibit personal growth.
- Adopting conscious consumption by always asking myself the questions "Where is my money going?" and "Who or what is impacted by this product or service?"
- Using my privilege to create space for different narratives.
- Adopting habits that are beneficial to people and the planet.
- Challenging the status quo by pushing back against stigmas and stereotypes.
- Investing time in community building.
- Speaking up against injustice and inequity.
- Actively working to dismantle systems of oppression.
- Cultivating joy and rest as an act of resistance and self-preservation.
- Learning to be unapologetic about saying no when I need to.
- Saying yes to the things that make me come alive.
- Trusting my intuition.
- Decolonizing my beauty and health routines.

CURATING MY VAN HOME

Minimalism is an embodied experience. The mindfulness and intentionality that I've learned along my journey extend to my physical space. Redefining minimalism has enabled me to curate an aesthetic that reflects my culture, my personality, and my unique sense of style. Every item in my home is intentional and each piece serves a purpose.

In my van, redefining minimalism looks like bright colors, fabrics, and textures that represent the beauty of the African and Indian diasporas and my Caribbean roots. It looks like a vibrant wardrobe, like tiny art pieces collected from community members along my travels, like an assortment of funky, chunky earrings displayed as decor and for easy storage and access.

It looks like an apothecary of DIY beauty products—deodorant, coffee scrub, beauty oils, and hair treatments. It looks like a low-waste pantry of mismatched, upcycled, and thrifted jars, always stocked with my favorite bulk goods. It looks like an overabundance of gear used to power our digital nomad life.

At the centerpiece of my tiny kitchen lives a bold and flamboyant spice collection for cooking up fiery cultural dishes that are bursting with flavors of my childhood. Preparing a meal in my cast-iron pot or pan is reminiscent of my grandma's fireside cooking. The knickknacks adorning my dash serve as little reminders of the places I've been and the journeys I've made in my van home.

I've found joy in transforming my van into a safe space, a sanctuary that is representative of me and all the intersections I navigate. Since leaving New Orleans, I've unapologetically re-created myself in this van more times than I can count. Through this process, I've come to know that minimalism isn't a standard to live up to; it's a commitment to a simpler and ethical lifestyle that is unique to you, one that brings you joy and peace.

Minimalism is daring to create the life you want to live. It's aligning with your values and living authentically. There is no right or wrong way to practice minimalism—it's a personal journey. How that unfolds in your life will look different than the way it did in mine, but don't let that fear of the unknown stop you.

A SIMPLE GUIDE FOR DOWNSIZING & MOVING INTO YOUR VAN

Downsizing your life to fit into a van can feel overwhelming at first, but once you get started, it can be liberating. Remember, embracing minimalism is not a one-and-done activity, it's an experiment in what is enough. To quote Christine Platt, the Afrominimalist, "minimalism is a beautiful dance between needs and wants."

The process of downsizing takes time, patience, and intentionality. Here are a few tips to help you get started.

DECLUTTER AS SOON AS POSSIBLE (BUT TAKE YOUR TIME)

Don't wait until you have your van to start. Pace yourself and gradually go through your possessions so you don't feel overwhelmed. Shed the first layer by decluttering and organizing your space. Think of this act as a primer to letting go of possessions you no longer need. It's also a great opportunity to identify the items you value that you want to bring with you into vanlife. There are no set rules, but here are a few methods that worked for me.

One-thing method: Look around your space for things that no longer serve you. Let go of one item at a time: this could be one item per day, one per week, or one per month.

Chunking method: Eat the proverbial elephant one bite at a time. Break your space down into smaller sections. You can separate it by category (books, clothes, art supplies, records, etc.) or take it room by room. You can even separate each section into smaller sections. For example, your closet can be broken down into clothes, shoes, jewelry, etc. Let go of items that no longer bring you joy.

Boxing method: As you go through your day-to-day life, take notice of things you no longer use. Put these items in a box, and when the box is full, close it up and send it away. It helps to determine early on where these items will go so you're not just moving things from one place to the next. Label the boxes: keep, donate, gift, trash, and sell.

TAKE INVENTORY

This is a twofold task, both physical and mental. In the process of downsizing, I've found that it's always helpful to assess where you're at before, during, and after. Write it down.

Physical: Go through your space and make a list of everything you own. Take note of how long it's been since you last used each item. Write down how it makes you feel. Does it bring you joy? Does it make your life easier in some way? A good rule of thumb is that if the answer to these questions is no, or if you haven't used it in the past year, let it go. And for items that elicit a yes to these questions, consider if it's something that you would like to bring with you into your new van home, if it will be useful and practical, and of course, if it will fit in the van.

Mental: Make a list of why you want to live vanlife (see question prompts in Chapter 2). Focus on what you need or hope to gain from this lifestyle. Maybe you want to save money and pay off student debt, live a more simplistic life, or see the country. Maybe you lost your job and want to live more frugally. Whatever it may be, put it on paper and visualize the reasons. These are the things that will keep you going when the journey gets tough and they can also serve as a reminder of what truly matters to you.

DOWNSIZE YOUR EXPENSES & BUDGET FOR VANLIFE

Downsizing isn't just about getting rid of possessions. Taking steps to eliminate bills, reduce expenses, and create a budget before you move into your rig can go a long way in ensuring a smooth transition into vanlife, especially if financial uncertainty is a concern.

Downsize expenses:

- Make a list of all your bills and expenses for one month. Highlight anything that is unnecessary or that you may be able to reduce.

- Be mindful of monthly subscriptions, as they're a big culprit in sneakily draining funds. Be it a $2.99 app or your membership in the jelly of the month club, it all adds up at the end of every month.

- Minimize eating out. Cook and eat at home, and definitely skip the coffee shop, as those five-dollar lattes add up quickly.

- Make a plan to pay off debt. Consolidate credit card debt onto one low-interest card. Pay off high-interest debt first.

- Budget for vanlife by anticipating what your expenses will be based on your lifestyle and activities. If you're traveling full-time, food and fuel will likely be the biggest costs.

- If you can, set aside some funds for possible breakdowns and other emergencies.

MEASURE OUT YOUR NEW SPACE

- If you have your rig, measure your space and visualize how things will fit inside of it. Think about what's important to you and what you want your new space to provide.

- Experiment by packing items into designated spaces and rearrange to find what fits where best.

- Consider your lifestyle when packing gear and clothes. What activities are you interested in? How much space do you need for gear? What varying climates will you experience?

- Do a test run. When you've packed your rig to your liking, take a trip and reevaluate. Are there things you could do without? Are there things you didn't consider that you may need? Is there a way to make your space more efficient and functional?

ADOPT LOW-WASTE HABITS

Living in a van forces you to confront how much waste you create on a daily basis, since there isn't a garbage truck coming to pick up your trash and haul it away for you. You alone are responsible for collecting and disposing of your trash regularly. Adopting low-waste habits before you move into your rig will help make the transition into a smaller space less overwhelming.

Buying more whole foods and bulk goods can help reduce packaging waste.

The ritual of preparing meals in a tiny kitchen is logistically challenging. Simplify cooking and experiment with healthy, one-pot meals.

Opting for reusables instead of disposables is a great way to reduce waste. Transfer dishes, pots, and pans you already own into your van rather than buying new or using disposables. As a menstruator, one of my biggest low-waste hacks was switching from tampons to a menstrual cup. There was an initial up-front investment, but in the long run, it has helped me reduce waste and save money, plus it's convenient for my active lifestyle.

Ultimately, our choices in life create profound changes in our hearts, our minds, and our world. For me, the journey to living a simpler, minimalist lifestyle means looking to the past to inform my choices in the present and the future. Within the four walls of my tan van, I'm continuously reevaluating my consumption and recommitting to living authentically.

CHAPTER 5

Essential Vanlife
Starter Kit

Now that you have a better understanding of how to downsize and move into a van, let's talk about some of the things you'll need to live on the road.

With a few simple modifications and additions, any vehicle can be transformed into an effective home-on-wheels. I'm not talking about a full-blown van conversion here, but if you start with some basic essentials, they can get you where you envision—in your rig and on the road. There are a couple of reasons why:

Financial. For those of us on a budget, vanlife can be the vehicle to reduce expenses and save money. But campervan conversions can be expensive and time-consuming. By starting with the basics, you can move into your rig quickly with minimal investment and save up for your next rig or your own conversion.

Needs. Starting with the basics essentially gives you a "try before you buy" experience. Think of this as experimental, an opportunity to assess and understand your needs. I've spoken to countless vanlifers who've shared stories of costly renovations to their newly converted rigs after only a few months on the road because their needs changed.

In my seven years living this lifestyle, my needs have changed considerably. We started with a rig equipped with some fundamentals: a two-burner propane stove, a small sink, and a multifunctional table. Thanks to the previous owner, it also came with some things we didn't know we would need, like a fifty-watt solar panel, deep-cycle battery, and eight-hundred-watt inverter. This covered our basic needs at the time, but we quickly outgrew the setup as our vanlife evolved to include careers as digital nomads. As any vanlifer will tell you, what's considered "essential" varies from person to person. But the good thing is, you don't need to have it all figured out before you get started.

Yes, everyone's vanlife needs are unique; however, there are some essentials that remain constant across the board. Consider this your starter kit, consisting of the things that will sustain you during your vanlife discovery phase. We'll dive into the technical side of vanlife starting with the basics, and then I'll share some of the upgrades that can take your vanlife to the next level.

THE VANLIFE BARE NECESSITIES

Like I said, getting started in vanlife doesn't have to break the bank. In fact, there's a good chance you already have much of what you need, and the rest can likely be acquired on a budget or second-hand.

Maslow's Hierarchy of Needs tells us that we must satisfy our most primal needs before we can attend to the higher-level psychological needs of love, belonging, and esteem. Those basic needs are physiological (food, water, air, sleep, shelter, warmth) and safety (which I discuss in detail in a later chapter). So I guess John Lennon was wrong when he sang, "Love is all you need." Perhaps the song should go "Love is all you need, after you have food, water, air, sleep, shelter, warmth, and safety."

With that in mind, this vanlife starter kit includes the essentials to cover all your basic needs. Maslow would be proud.

A COMFORTABLE BED

The most obvious need in vanlife is a place to sleep. This could be an air mattress in the back of your SUV or a sleeping pad laid across your back seat. I've even seen some folks start out with a mattress on the floor of their empty van. Basically, you'll need something comfortable that will get you horizontal and let you stretch out. Take notes, because this is a great opportunity to get a feel for how you want to lay out your space.

WATER STORAGE

There is no life without water and vanlife is no exception. Unfortunately, for many of us, water is something we often take for granted when there's an unlimited supply flowing out of the tap. According to the USGS, the average person in the US uses eighty to one hundred gallons of water per day. In vanlife, it's ideal to limit that to one to two gallons per day for everything, including drinking, cooking, washing dishes, and washing ourselves. Reusable water jugs, ideally those with a five-to-seven-gallon capacity, provide a simple and effective water storage solution. I recommend carrying enough water to last a minimum of three to five days, or one jug per person.

FOOD STORAGE

- Dustin and I were fortunate that our rig came with a twelve-volt marine fridge, but you don't need a refrigerator to get started in vanlife. A hard cooler is sufficient to keep most perishable foods fresh. Pre-vanlife, Dustin and I did a few extended road trips, and our main food storage was a cooler. A friend recommended we pair our ice cubes with dry ice, which we wrapped in a cloth and laid at the bottom of the cooler. It extended the life of our ice cubes by an extra two days. In vanlife, that means fewer trips into town and less risk of perishables going bad.

  Pro Tip: Store ice cubes in extralarge ziplock bags to keep your food from being saturated. When the ice melts, use the water for washing dishes.

- Dry goods require far less maintenance, as they just need a secure place to rest without rolling around while you're driving. This could be as simple as a cardboard box or a milk crate.

COOKING EQUIPMENT

- A portable camping stove provides the option of cooking inside your van or outside. Most are foldable, compact, durable, and easy to store. If you enjoy cooking, a two-burner stove will provide more options. For folks who typically opt for quick or precooked meals, a single-burner stove may be sufficient.

- Cookware and dishware can be as simple as a pot and/or pan, one fork, one spoon, one plate, and one bowl. If there are two of you, double the dishware. Dustin and I have two of each in our van and when we have guests over for dinner, they bring their own.

BLANKETS & PILLOWS

Blankets provide warmth and pillows comfort. Your current pillow and blanket will do. My vanlife luxury on chilly nights is tucking a hot-water bottle under the covers for an added layer of warmth and comfort when I need it most.

TOILETRIES & PERSONAL HYGIENE

While Maslow didn't include this in his hierarchy, cleanliness is essential to health, and living in a van doesn't mean sacrificing hygiene. The toiletries and personal hygiene products you use on a daily basis can be transferred to your rig to maintain a personal care routine.

WASHBASIN

A washbasin is useful for washing dishes and washing yourself. A collapsible washbasin stores easily, or a rigid basin can double as additional storage in the van when not in use.

SOLAR SHOWER BAG

"How do you stay clean?" is one of the most common questions I get from people interested in vanlife. For me, nothing is better than a buck-naked shower out in nature. When we first started vanlife, I used an inexpensive solar shower bag. I'd fill it from a river or creek first thing in the morning and set it in the sun. Throughout the day the dark material of the bag would catch the sun's rays and warm the water. By late evening I'd have a hot shower.

ROADSIDE MAINTENANCE & RECOVERY KIT

Dustin and I have found ourselves broken down with no cell service in remote places more times than we can count. Fortunately, he's quite handy when it comes to mechanics. After seven years of breakdowns, I can confidently say he knows our van inside and out and can problem-solve us out of pretty much any situation, provided he has the right tools. So take his advice:

Dustin's Pro Tip: Keep a basic set of mechanic tools and recovery gear in your rig. At a minimum, carry a spare tire, jack and tire tool, tow strap, traction boards, jumper cables, socket set, crescent wrench and screwdrivers, and a good flashlight. You'll probably need all of these at some point. Keeping a spare key hidden somewhere on your rig is also a good idea in case you lock yourself out.

FIRE EXTINGUISHER

Just like in a stationary home, a fire extinguisher is an essential safety component in a van home. A carbon monoxide detector is also a must-have if you have propane in your rig.

FIRST AID KIT

- Many of us think it will never happen, but I always recommend preparing for worst-case scenarios. Dustin and I spend a lot of time off-grid and in the backcountry, where medical care is not easily accessible, so a good first aid kit is an essential safety component. In addition to basic first aid items such as bandages, gauze, and aspirin, our vanlife first aid kit includes trauma pads, burn dressings, a tourniquet, self-venting chest seals, a pressure bandage, moldable splint, and QuikClot gauze. We also keep a smaller pared-down version that we carry with us when we're hiking, backpacking, or engaging in other outdoor activities.

- Since we've added a furry riding partner to our vanlife, we keep a doggy first aid kit in the van as well. Our dog-specific first aid kit includes nonstick bandages, gauze, self-adhering tape, tweezers, magnifying glass, a soft muzzle, an inflatable cone, an oral syringe, hydrogen peroxide, antibiotic spray, and paw balm or paw pad ointment.

TROWEL OR SHOVEL

If you don't have a toilet in your rig, your go-to option is pooping outside. For this, you'll need a shovel or a trowel to dig a hole. A good rule of thumb when you have to go is to find a spot away from water sources and trails, dig a cathole six to eight inches deep, do your business, and fill the hole back up with dirt. Carry a small ziplock bag to pack your toilet paper out with you, as animals sometimes dig it up and leave nasty bits of TP scattered about.

BLACKOUT CURTAINS OR WINDOW COVERINGS

Living in a van means being exposed to the elements. But when I close the curtains in my van, it becomes my private, safe space. Blackout curtains also block outside light, providing better sleep quality. This is especially important if you're an urban vandweller.

LIGHTS

Often overlooked is the need for extra lighting at night, and relying on your vehicle's dome light is just asking for a dead battery. An alternate source of lighting such as a lantern, a flashlight, or a headlamp is essential for safety and convenience.

PERSONAL ESSENTIALS

We all have things that are essential to our daily lives and there is no reason those things shouldn't accompany us into vanlife. That may include a comfortable pair of slippers, a hat and sunglasses, vitamins and medication, or your favorite Snuggie. Living a life of simplicity and minimalism is about what you value and what brings you joy.

ESSENTIAL VANLIFE UPGRADES

Now that those basic needs are met, you can begin to address more specific needs and wants. These upgrades can add comfort and convenience and take your vanlife to the next level.

POWER SETUP

There are several options for powering your vanlife. The most common setup includes one or more solar panels and a deep cycle battery, paired with a twelve-volt power inverter. It took us a few years to get this dialed in, but once we did, it transformed our van into a fully functional mobile office. A simpler option that can still elevate your power setup is a portable power station and solar panel. It can be less expensive and there's no installation required.

TWELVE-VOLT FRIDGE

A good power setup makes it possible to add a refrigerator to your rig. This eliminates the hassle of keeping ice handy and worrying about perishables going bad. The addition of this modern cooling device means you can store more food for longer and make fewer trips for supplies.

SINK & WATER PUMP

Running water is a convenience many people take for granted until they've lived in a van. A limited supply and regular quest to replenish quickly puts things into perspective. The addition of a foot-powered water pump gives control over how much flows through the tap, making it easy to conserve water. Some rigs even have gray water holding tanks. Gray water is the runoff from washing our bodies, our dishes, our clothes—basically any wastewater that's not from the toilet. Methods for disposing gray water vary based on the state, city, or municipality you're in; when in doubt, use a designated dump station for disposal.

WATER FILTRATION

Water filtration can be as convenient as an inline filter between your water storage and your tap, or as simple as a dispenser or pitcher with replaceable filters. With a good filter, you can collect water from practically any source or tap. Keep in mind, there are many types of filters that remove bacteria and protozoa and water purifiers that remove viruses. Do your research and be sure to get the proper filter for your needs.

ELECTRIC FAN

In my vanlife, we move with the seasons, but still, there are times when the van becomes too hot for comfort. This is where an electric fan comes in handy. We have two twelve-volt fans, one clipped to the dash (our version of air-conditioning), and a small box fan with a low power draw to cool the cabin.

AWNING

This is one of the best and simplest upgrades we've made to our van. An awning provides shade from the sun, shelter from the rain, and doubles the size of our living area by giving us

a comfortable space outside the van no matter the weather.

PROPANE HEATER

I'm not a fan of cold weather—I'm from the tropics, for crying out loud. I'm accustomed to warmer temps. When the temperature drops below sixty degrees, I'm thankful I have a heater. Ours is a propane-fired furnace installed beneath the bench seat, but this can be as simple as a portable Mr. Buddy heater. I recommend propane because electric heaters draw a lot of power.

dinner in the dark. Twelve-volt LED strip lights are inexpensive, easy to install, and draw minimal power. You can even get dimmable or multicolored, depending on how you like to get down.

SAFE OR LOCKBOX

A secure place to store valuables affords peace of mind when you're away from your rig. You don't need a Fort Knox–level safe—any lockbox can be sufficient, as long as it can be bolted to the floor.

As with anything in life, you don't have to have it all figured out right when you start. It's been seven-plus years on the road with Irie, and we're still tweaking, still growing, still evolving as our needs change. Three years in, we pulled over on a dusty Texas highway, Amara hopped on, and we became a pack. As a result, some of our needs and desires took a back seat as we prioritized the needs and comforts of another being in our care. But to be honest, it doesn't feel like I gave up anything. Being a dog mom has brought so much joy and adventure into my life on the road. Which is part of the beauty of vanlife: it leaves you room to go with the flow, to be shaped and molded, and can lead to some of the most extraordinary experiences. For me, vanlife is an experiment. It's a never-ending canvas and we're the artists. And we get to create and re-create as many times as we want.

PORTABLE TOILET

This is a hotly debated topic in vanlife circles: toilet or no toilet. For some, a toilet is a necessity, while for others it's a luxury. I do not have a toilet in my van because, with two humans and a dog sharing eighty square feet, we just don't have the space. But if we had a larger rig, I would definitely consider adding a composting toilet.

OVERHEAD LIGHTING

Proper lighting is another amenity taken for granted until you find yourself trying to cook

CHAPTER 6

Travel & Camping

On April 19, 2016, just before dark, we quietly rolled through the campground entrance.

The cool mountain air of Hot Springs National Park, Arkansas, provided a welcome reprieve from the Louisiana humidity that had permeated the van as we traversed the state. With no host on duty to collect our fee, we carefully crept into the first empty spot we found.

As the adrenaline of the day began to wear off, Dustin and I sat quietly in the front seat, taking in the stillness around us. I'm not sure how I expected our first night in the van to go, or if I had considered it at all before this point. Until that moment, all my time and energy had been wrapped up in the details of what we would need for our year on the road. Finally, we turned and looked at each other, the nervous energy swelling in the air so thick you could cut it with a knife. Dustin broke the silence: "Let's pop the top and settle in."

Standing side by side in the space that doubles as our kitchen, living room, and dining room, we pushed with all the force we could muster, raising the top slowly into position, the crossbar snap-

ping into place to support the weight. I exhaled with a sigh. *It's official*, I thought, *this is our new home*. With that, a mix of pride, gratitude, and anxiety flooded my mind like a wave. As I lingered for a moment, attempting to process that medley of emotions, Dustin swiveled the front passenger seat around, opening up our living space.

I uncorked a bottle of wine and pulled out the collapsible silicone cups that I had bought, thinking they would save space (it turns out they were ridiculous, flimsy, and completely unnecessary, but lesson learned). I poured two glasses and handed one to Dustin as I sat down next to him on the bench seat. My first sip of wine tasted like a mix of fear and freedom; maybe it was the emotions of our first day in vanlife, or maybe that's just how wine tastes out of a silicone cup.

The next few moments passed in what felt like an eternity. I had spent months preparing for vanlife, but I couldn't have accounted for what it would feel like when I finally closed the door on a life that seemed all but written out for me and

slid open a new door to a life entirely unscripted. For the first time, I had no agenda, no work the next morning, no social invitations, no idea what lay ahead; it was terrifying. Finally, I looked at Dustin and said, "What's next?" He put his arm around me, pulled me in closer, and calmly whispered, "I don't know, but the good thing is, we don't have to figure it out right now." For the rest of the evening we sipped in silence.

Falling asleep that night was a feat. I lay in my loft bed staring at the ceiling, my head swirling with anxious thoughts of tomorrow. The mellow glow of the moon through my blue canvas window served to soothe my racing mind. I awoke the next morning to the bright trill of a mockingbird. As my eyes opened and the awareness of my surroundings slowly returned, I felt a smile grow wide on my face, excitement brewing inside. From the bench seat below I heard a rustle:

"Hey, you up?" Dustin asked, brimming with eagerness. "Let's hit the road."

REIMAGINING TRAVEL

That first day we drove four hundred miles across Louisiana to get to our destination. Farms and fields and forests flashed by in a haze of obscurity, our minds focused on the end goal with little concern for what we might experience along the way. This was our pace for much of our first year on the road—we were caught up with the urge to see it all. Fortunately, the way Dustin and I travel now has changed a lot since back then.

Even though we didn't have a blueprint for our life on the road, I still had an idea as to how things would probably go. I thought I'd have some epiphany early on that would open my eyes and provide answers to all my questions. But over the years, I've learned that travel isn't some mystical medicine that transforms you. It does, however, present opportunities to learn more about the world and about yourself. From leaving my country at seventeen, to adopting vanlife years later, travel has continuously pushed me out of my comfort zone and connected me to people and cultures I otherwise would never have experienced. It has opened my mind and taught me that there is no one way to live. Breaking free of the "destination mindset" was my first step to slowing down and opening myself up to new experiences.

Burnt-out from our fast-paced first year of vanlife, Dustin and I took an impromptu trip to Southeast Asia to disconnect and recharge. This was my first time as an international tourist and it was a swift lesson in the unsustainable effects of the social phenomenon of mass tourism—cultural commodification, environmental degradation, pollution, overcrowding, waste problems, exploitation of local peoples. Those six months backpacking abroad fundamentally changed me and taught me the kind of traveler I want to be. And I brought those lessons back home with me.

While it may seem simplistic, bar none, adopting slow travel has been the most impactful shift that I've made in my life on the road and my best piece of advice for new and aspiring vanlifers. Taken literally, slow travel simply means slowing down your travels or traveling slowly. The idea is that rather than rushing from place to place, you spend all your allotted time in one city, town, or area. Imagine visiting a place and learning it so well, you could actually be a tour guide. That's the essence of slow travel in a nutshell and for many people, myself included, it's synonymous with sustainable travel.

Helpful and essential apps for road travel*

iOverlander: This is the app we utilize the most on the road for planning our travels. It's a map-based app with a robust database of user-generated listings and reviews for free and developed camping, as well as resources like propane, water fill, showers, and much more. There is no verification or assurance of the quality or legality of the sites, so read the reviews, do your due diligence, and use your best judgment.

The Native Land app (and website Native-land.ca): A resource to learn the names of the Indigenous peoples whose land we're camping and recreating on (more on that later), the app also provides information about the history, cultures, and languages of different tribes. It's an important part of my travel arsenal.

Outdoorsy Black Women: I'm a proud member of the OBW community. This app was founded and created by a friend and fellow road traveler. It's a social network that empowers Black women in various niches in road travel and the outdoors to connect, collaborate, and build community.

Diversify Vanlife Discord server: Created as an alternative to mainstream social media platforms, the DV Discord server is not governed by algorithms. It's a safe space for the DV community and for nomads, road travelers, and outdoor enthusiasts at all intersections and from all walks of life to show up authentically, connect, and collaborate.

Campendium: We use Campendium whenever we're looking for a developed campground with amenities. It's heavily weighted toward the RV community, though it does have a growing collection of dispersed campsites. While its database of free camping options is not as robust as iOverlander, its locations and reviews are more trustworthy. While Campendium is free to use, it also has premium features that can be unlocked by purchasing a subscription. Those features include the ability to search by cell coverage and map overlays showing the locations of public lands.

GasBuddy: This was an essential app for Dustin and me even before vanlife. Fuel is our biggest expense on the road, so it's great being able to compare gas prices. And knowing where gas stations are located on our route gives us the ability to plan our stops accordingly.

FreeRoam: Another campsite search app, this one features a social component, allowing users to connect with other road travelers within the app. You can also view maps based on cell phone coverage, which we've found helpful when boondocking.

* See https://diversifyvanlife.com/essential-apps/.

SLOW TRAVEL AS A FORM OF RADICAL RESISTANCE

As a Black woman, the misguided narrative that I must be strong and invulnerable in spite of obstacles has followed me all my life—and in turn, affected my ability to foster authenticity. I frequently glorified busyness as an indicator of my self-worth and wore my stresses like a badge of honor. It wasn't until life on the road in my slow, classic rig that I grasped the severity of society's addiction to rushing. Have you ever had someone try to run you off the road for going fifty-five miles per hour? I have, and it's one reason why Dustin and I opt for back roads and small towns over interstates and big cities. America's hurrying culture is so deeply ingrained that many of us never realize we're perpetually in a rush.

Practicing slow travel as an intentional way of life means releasing expectations and opening yourself up to a new way of seeing the world. It also means accepting experiences for what they are, rather than imparting our own ideas of what they should be. The way I see it, vanlife is an act of resistance. It's a challenge to the status quo. If you have the privilege to choose this lifestyle, then you also have a responsibility to work toward positive change for all people and the planet.

When we slow down our road travels, we open

- Supporting Black, Indigenous, and other marginalized communities, including the unhoused.

- Intentionally seeking out and supporting Black and Indigenous-owned businesses, as well as LGBTQIA+ and other POC-owned businesses and amplifying them on my platforms.

- Genuinely engaging with and supporting local businesses during my travels.

- Staying informed of the power dynamics and diversity in my destinations.

- Seeking out challenging cultural and spiritual experiences and in doing so, being intentional to not center myself or burden the individuals of this culture.

- Seeking to support local Indigenous guides for services whenever possible.

- Taking time to lend my expertise where I can and identifying grassroots initiatives that give financial donations. Every dollar counts.

- Using my voice and platform in support of BIPOC leaders in the vanlife, road travel, and outdoor communities.

- Being an antiracist traveler.

- Creating a plan on how I will apply what I've learned in my life.

- Redefining the whitewashed narratives of the outdoors, vanlife, and slow travel.

ourselves up to learning about different cultures, land, people, and ways of living. We create room for unlearning biases and adopting habits that are more aligned with our values. For me, one key commitment in this fight is promoting socially conscious consumption. On our travels, Dustin and I put our money where our values are, because reimagining society requires collective and individual action and solidarity. Ask yourself, how am I creating positive change in my community as a road traveler and/or outdoorist?

My answer to that question goes something like this. I am creating positive change as a road traveler by:

NATIVE LAND

I will always remember my first national park experience at Great Smoky Mountains National Park in Tennessee. The scenic vistas and sweeping mountain views took my breath away. The bold silhouettes of these ancient giants, shrouded in mist, seemed to be etched into the sky. We hiked for a few days on well-worn trails through old-growth forests, traversed rushing mountain streams, took ice-cold plunges in shallow pools of cascading waterfalls, ate lunch in meadows carpeted with wildflowers, scrambled up and down scree fields laden with loose rocks and boulders, and slept under a blanket of stars. Daily wildlife sightings provided welcome excitement—elk, white-tailed deer, an abundance of birds, the occasional coyote. I even had my first black bear encounter.

This was the trip that reconnected me with my passion for nature and the outdoors and resurrected my dream of traveling the country in a van. Since that day, I've explored dozens of national parks across the US—braved the dusty desert of Death Valley, hugged towering redwood trees in Northern California, photographed wolves in Yellowstone, stargazed among the sandstone spires of Canyonlands in Utah. In fact, for the vast majority of my vanlife journey, Irie's wheels have traversed public lands as the places where we work, recreate, and camp.

Public lands are areas of land and water that are managed by government agencies and paid for with tax dollars. These include lands managed by the National Park Service (NPS), Bureau of Land Management (BLM), the Forest Service (FS), and Fish and Wildlife Service (FWS). As per publiclands.com, combined, these agencies manage 640 million acres of land (26.6 percent of the land in the US). Public lands offer countless opportunities for individuals to access natural spaces for outdoor recreation, leisure, health, or other reasons.

But there is an ugly history behind the formation of public lands that is important for us to acknowledge. These areas were designated only after the violent removal of Indigenous peoples by the US government. Millions of acres of land, stolen in the name of "preservation and conservation," while US policies continue to exclude and erase the true history of the land and the Indigenous peoples who have lived and continue to live on it. Prior to European colonization, many Indigenous Nations had vibrant communities, trade routes, and

When we verbalize or write the original Indigenous names of the lands beneath our wheels or feet, we are attempting to access and empathize with the generational trauma and grief felt by Native communities for centuries. We are momentarily paying respect, mourning, and showing evidence of an effort to unlearn colonial legacy.

—Wynnē Weddell, Diversify Vanlife

alliances that connected Inuit Nunaat in so-called Canada and Alaska to the Great Plains of the contiguous United States to beyond the border with Mexico. Indigenous peoples are still here and thriving, despite genocide, relocation, assimilation, and ongoing policies that dispossess them of their rights to ancestral land, water, and clean air.

As non-Native road travelers and outdoorists, we must recognize the problematic history of the creation of America's public lands and the continued abuse toward Native peoples, and work to create an inclusive outdoors with the collaboration of Indigenous leadership. Acknowledging whose land you're camping and recreating on is a good first step in recognizing the cultural and literal genocide that occurred on the land now known as the US. It also serves to raise awareness that the US government has broken every treaty made with Indigenous peoples in the past and is now trying to nullify them. It's also important to recognize that land justice for Native people will not arise from a land acknowledgment. Beyond that, learn the true history of the original inhabitants of the land and share what you've learned with others.

Ways to support Indigenous communities beyond land acknowledgments:

○ Learn the history of the land you're camping and recreating on. The Native Land app (and website Native-land.ca) is a great resource to help you get started.

○ Support the #LandBack movement.

○ Follow up with financial, educational, and political support.

○ Follow Indigenous leaders online and on social media.

○ Visit Indigenous-curated museums, restaurants, and small businesses.

○ Contact grassroots organizations and tribes online or in person to determine how to contribute to locally driven initiatives.

○ Find out what development projects are being proposed on Indigenous "public" lands and do your homework to determine how to support Indigenous peoples politically.

WHERE DO YOU GO WHEN YOU CAN GO ANYWHERE?

Vanlife gives us the flexibility to travel almost anywhere we want in continental North America, provided we have the resources. Imagine having all the time in the world and the ability to design your life based on what brings you joy and pleasure. So where would you go?

Many vanlifers travel with the seasons. As our Irie doesn't have air-conditioning, and since neither of us is fond of cold climates, Dustin and I typically look for places that are seventy-five degrees and sunny. In the spring, we slowly make our way north to cooler climates, so by the time the summer heat kicks in, we find ourselves in spots like the Eastern Sierra Mountains or the big sky country of Montana. When Old Man Winter rears his head again, we head south to warmer locales like Baja, Mexico. But that's just our style. Some vanlifers travel like us, avoiding the extremes, while others relish the snow and travel with the intention of chasing powder.

This type of intentionality speaks to two driving factors that dictate the movement of vanlifers: camping and outdoor recreation. Climbing, surfing, skiing, kayaking, mountain biking; you name the activity and there's a vanlifer who plans their travels around it. Public lands provide the setting for many of these outdoor activities, and it's no coincidence that they also provide an abundance of camping options. There are many options for camping in your rig, but they all fall into one of three categories: developed camping, dispersed camping, and stealth camping.

Developed Camping is the act of camping in established and maintained campgrounds with designated sites.

The most popular type of camping is developed camping. RV parks, national and state parks, and public and privately owned campgrounds are some of the places you can find developed camping. We've stayed in every type of developed campground, from those with only basic amenities like a picnic table, fire ring, and pit toilet to premium campgrounds with showers, laundry, electricity, Wi-Fi, potable water, and more. We've even gotten "bougie" a time or two and splurged on campgrounds with mineral springs and spa packages. We typically partake in developed camping on occasions when we need premium amenities or want to explore a national park with our van.

PROS & CONS OF DEVELOPED CAMPING

Pros:

◦ **Discoverability:** Developed campgrounds are easier to find through many apps and online resources, including Google Maps. Sometimes you can reserve your site before you arrive.

◦ **Amenities:** Many developed campgrounds include amenities such as electricity, running water, toilets (vault or pit toilets if rural/primitive), showers, fire ring, grill, level surface, trash cans, recycling, and more.

◦ **Clean and secure:** Developed campgrounds often have a camp host who lives onsite and provides administration, security, and maintenance. So they're typically safer and cleaner than dispersed campgrounds.

Cons:

◦ Many developed campgrounds charge a fee.

◦ They often require a reservation and have designated check-in and check-out times.

◦ Dogs/pets must always be leashed.

◦ The minimal separation between sites means less privacy and close neighbors, which may not be a good thing.

Dispersed Camping is the act of camping on public lands outside of designated campgrounds.

Dispersed camping is remote, secluded, and free, which is why it's the type of camping that Dustin and I most frequently engage in. One reason why public lands are popular among road travelers is that free camping outside of established campgrounds is allowed. Dispersed camping gives us the option of choosing our own campsite. I love the feeling of turning off the highway onto a dirt road in a national forest or BLM area and driving deep into the woods or miles through the desert searching for our ideal campsite. While that means we'll find no amenities, and often no cell service, it also means no neighbors, no light pollution, and no noise pollution; just trees, wildlife, blue skies, a blanket of stars, and miles and miles of exploration.

If getting outdoors among nature is the goal, then dispersed camping on public lands is a great option. Keep in mind, however, that having no amenities means you have to bring everything you need with you and carry everything back out with you as well, including trash.

HOW TO SELECT A DISPERSED CAMPSITE

When you're out in nature, away from developed campgrounds, it may seem like no rules apply, but it's important to follow a few guidelines:

- Even if no fees apply for the area you're camping in, you may need a fire or camping permit. Be sure to check with the local ranger station or office.

- Park your van/car/bus/RV at least two hundred feet away from water sources to prevent runoff and to give local wildlife safe access to water sources.

- Check for fire restrictions before you travel to remote areas, as cell service may be limited. This includes learning if campfires or open stoves are permitted—during the dry season in many parts of the country, drought conditions are severe and no flames of any sort are allowed.

- Be prepared to carry all your trash out with you.

- Bring enough drinking water, especially in dry or desert areas.

- Be prepared to camp on bare, hard-packed surfaces.

- To find a secluded spot, you may have to drive farther down a road to get away from the crowds. Be careful, as most of the time these roads are not maintained. Sometimes it's worth getting out and walking to see if it's safe to drive on.

- Many public lands have a fourteen-day camping limit. After that time, you must move at least twenty-five miles away before finding a new dispersed area to camp. This is to prevent damage to sensitive resources that can be caused by continual use.

PROS & CONS OF DISPERSED CAMPING

Pros:

- It's free!
- Plenty of options for camping, so you can keep driving until you find a spot you like.
- Spectacular scenery in the daytime and a blanket of stars at night.
- Dogs can run free.
- No noisy neighbors.
- Privacy.
- Stay for as long as you like (typically up to fourteen days).
- Did I mention, it's free!?!?

Cons:

- No amenities, such as toilets or running water.
- The remote nature means no cell service in many locations.
- It's sometimes difficult determining where you're allowed to camp, as private land and public lands sometimes intersect. Pay attention to No Trespassing signs.
- Campsites are not guaranteed. We've arrived at places where the sites were all taken, or the only available sites were open to the elements or the ground was too uneven to camp on.
- You never know what you're going to get until you get there.

Stealth Camping is the act of secretly camping in unestablished locations, with the goal of going undetected.

Early in our vanlife, I thought we'd have more opportunities to explore cities that were on our bucket list, to visit museums in DC, attend concerts in New York City. But living in a van and camping in cities is much more complicated. And when we added a German Shepherd companion who "warns" anyone if they get too close, stealth camping in cities was no longer an option.

Stealth camping refers to sleeping in your van in an urban setting without drawing attention to yourself. This can be alongside a city or residential street or in a quiet parking lot—the point is to go undetected. I know—that kind of sounds like something from a spy movie (and there are probably some stealthy spy vans on corner blocks in your city hiding in plain sight). But as thrilling as it may seem, stealth camping works better for some van types than others. My Irie, for example, is about as conspicuous as an elephant in a china shop. She sticks out because she's an obvious campervan, outfitted for off-grid living, complete with solar panels on the roof, a cell phone booster antenna, a trash carrier and Hula-Hoops on the back, and curtains on the windows. The best stealth camping rigs are inconspicuous: white cargo vans, Sprinters, ProMasters, converted delivery vans, and good ole minivans.

PROS & CONS OF STEALTH CAMPING

Pros:
- Convenient location if you need to be in a city.
- Access to resources.

Cons:
- Risk of being asked to leave.
- Risk of being ticketed if camped illegally.
- Can be bright and/or noisy.
- Inconvenient if you have a pet or don't have a toilet in your rig.
- Can leave you vulnerable to theft and vandalism.

But this urban camping is not without risks. If you find yourself in a place where overnight parking is prohibited (or if there are nosy neighbors), you may be asked to leave or even given a ticket. A good practice is to scout your location in advance, then drive to a public area such as a nearby park to take care of any business for the evening: cooking, eating dinner, doing dishes, washing up, walking the dog, etc. That way, when you get to "camp" you'll only need to draw the curtains and get in bed, and you'll have less risk of drawing attention to yourself.

Slowing down my road travels and being more intentional with the way I interact with the land and people has deepened my relationship with myself and the world. Whether I'm boondocking off-grid, sharing a campground with strangers, or stealth camping on a city street, I allow myself moments to pause, to connect a bit deeper, to stay a little longer, to learn something new about the place I'm visiting. For me, vanlife and reimagining travel in this old rig is a soulful experience.

CHAPTER 7

Being Safe on the Road

The world is a scary place.

At least, that's what I learned growing up in my tiny rural village in Trinidad. Don't talk to strangers. Don't go anywhere alone because danger lurks around every corner. Don't try anything different. These fearful narratives were so deeply ingrained in my family and community that I seldom experienced anything outside of the limits of my village. When I left Trinidad for the US, I didn't know how to act. On one side, I felt the pull of my newfound independence, leading me to embrace all the new experiences and, on the other, the conditions of my upbringing were ordering me to play it safe. Adapting meant I had to renegotiate what fears were mine and which ones didn't belong to me. It was a process of unlearning and rewiring, defining for myself what risks I was willing to take and not letting the fear of others keep me from living life on my own terms.

Whenever we step out of our homes—whether it's a stationary house, an apartment, or a van on the road—we open ourselves up to numerous risks that can affect our safety. Most of these threats we accept as a normal part of life, and, from an early age, we learn to protect and defend ourselves accordingly. We are wired with a desire to stay safe—we look both ways before crossing the street, wear a seatbelt and drive carefully, and avoid dark alleys at night.

But when living in a van, you're forced to take these concerns one step further. There are some unique questions that come up for individuals who want to live in a van on the road, like:

- Where do I park?

- Where do I sleep at night?

- How do I find potable water and other basic resources?

- Where do I find community?

While these are important for everyone, for certain groups of humans—solo travelers including women and gender nonconforming people, BIPOC, people with disabilities, LGBTQIA+

individuals, and people navigating multiple intersections—the conversation around safety elicits a heightened level of anxiety. In Chapter 2, I shared how *The Negro Motorist Green Book* was a key tool for Black travelers seeking safety in the early-to-mid-twentieth century. The publication ceased after the passage of the Civil Rights Act of 1964, thus fulfilling Victor Hugo Green's dream of a day when the guide would no longer be needed. However, for Black people on the road today, many of the dangers that the *Green Book* addressed—the risk of driving at night, getting to where you're going before sundown, and places with a high likelihood of harassment and police interaction—remain valid. These historical factors—police violence, profiling, xenophobia, racism, and other "isms"—play a significant role in our sense of safety.

As a Black-identifying, queer woman and first-generation immigrant, feeling safe on the road is not a sure thing: it's never a given in the small towns of rural America—locales where Confederate flags fly proudly—or in cities where statues of slave owners stand tall on street corners bearing the names of colonizers. Around every corner in this great nation, I feel a foreboding sense of fear and anger, instilling a feeling that I will never truly be welcome here. But never was this more evident than during the 2020 election period.

Dustin and I sat broken down at the side of the road near a small New Mexico town when a pickup truck flying a large American flag sped by. A middle-aged-looking white man hanging out the passenger-side window shouted racial slurs and profanities, followed by a political rallying cry: "Trump 2020!" Terrified, I locked myself in the van until the tow truck arrived.

This snapshot from the road during a tumultuous time reminds me of the thin line between safety and vulnerability that we all walk, especially when living a mobile life. As a once-in-a-century pandemic raged and the political and social divide deepened, media outlets went to war against one another, and "fake news" spread like wildfire across social media. In cities across the country, calls for justice were met with police batons and tear gas. For every Black Lives Matter bumper sticker, there was a lawn decorated with an All Lives Matter yard sign. Friends on the road reluctantly admitted to removing BLM stickers from their vans, fearing vigilante vandalism, as "proud boys" in pickup trucks patrolled the roads of rural America with seeming impunity. Unfortunately, for those of us with melanated skin, blending in isn't as easy as removing a sticker.

PSYCHOLOGICAL SAFETY MATTERS

A critical first step for the well-being of anyone on the road is safety. Being safe and feeling safe go together. For me, they're equally important.

Coined by Harvard Business School professor Dr. Amy Edmondson, psychological safety is described as "a belief that one will not be punished or humiliated for speaking up with ideas, questions, concerns, or mistakes." For those of us living on the road, psychological safety also entails believing that we are secure in our environment—safe from vandalism, safe to step outside at night, welcomed, included, and represented in the physical spaces we inhabit, and welcomed in our communities, both virtual and in person.

Feeling safe in our homes, workplaces, and communities is important. And as we reimagine our ideas of home and community in vanlife, it's important that we also broaden our concept of safety and what this means for different groups of people within the spaces we create.

Likewise, our sense of safety affects our quality of sleep. To reach a level of deep sleep, it's important to feel safe enough to let your guard down. But that's not always easy on the road, especially for BIPOC and LGBTQIA+ individuals. And for those who are forced into this lifestyle, insecurity is felt even more deeply. As I've grown into my life on the road, I've found that my quality of sleep is intricately linked to how safe I feel. And as the environment outside my van bedroom changes, so too does my level of safety and comfort. On the road, these adaptations often occur depending on my location; whether I'm stealth camping in a city, alone in a remote place in the backcountry, in a campground among strangers, or surrounded by friends and community, I have different trigger points and gut reactions.

In my first few months in the van, my sense of security was severely tested through the four tin walls of Irie. REM sleep was rare. Not having a toilet in my van meant late-night trips into the darkness, where every cackle, chirp, howl, or scurry made me gasp in fear. The yipping of coyotes sent me into a panicked frenzy, thinking a creature of the night might snatch me up and carry me away when I squatted down to pee. Of course, this was all in my head, and over time, I've worked through these natural fears.

I've come to feel a deep sense of safety and security with nature as my backyard. That's not to say camping in nature doesn't offer occasional dangers, but as I spend more time outside and embrace the discomfort of a new way of living, the scary and unfamiliar sounds outside my van have become the white noise that soothes me to sleep at night.

These remote, natural settings are now the backdrop for much of my vanlife journey. I typically try to avoid cities in favor of a dispersed campsite, but it's not always possible. I remember vividly my first urban camping experience. The radiating, artificial glow from the streetlight, the cacophony of sounds of the city—the hum of traffic on the freeway, the occasional ambulance wailing, buses moaning and screeching to a halt, dogs barking, and voices of pedestrians on the sidewalk—all contributed to a night of restlessness. When I did manage to sleep, I dreamt of vandals breaking in or police knocking on the window and ordering us out at gunpoint. I even had visions of the van rolling down a hill and tow trucks whisking us away. The urban orchestra outside weaved a narrative in my subconscious mind, distorting and magnifying my angst.

Though Dustin and I have spent numerous nights camped on residential streets and in parking lots, my sense of safety while parked in cities hasn't strengthened. It doesn't help that Irie isn't exactly a stealthy van either. As I mentioned before, her solar panels, cargo box, and other accoutrements are a dead giveaway that she's a lived-in rig, and this makes us a target for law enforcement, pugnacious homeowners, shady characters, and everything in between.

I've learned to accept that there will be times in my life on the road when I'll need to spend a discreet night sleeping on a city street. And I am ever thankful for the privilege of choosing when, where, and how I engage in urban vanlife. Many vehicle dwellers, including the unhoused, don't have the luxury of camping in nature or of moving on to more vanlife-friendly cities. As more cities pass laws prohibiting vehicle habitation, those most vulnerable in our communities are pushed farther into the margins. This is a subject we need to talk about, and these are the vanlifers who need support and community more than anyone.

Safety is typically viewed as a tangible, physical thing, but our feeling of safety is often what shapes our experiences. Much of what makes vanlife an exciting and intriguing lifestyle—an ever-changing environment, new places, new people—also contributes to feelings of insecurity, especially when it comes to where we lay our heads at night. And while the fears and anxieties I experience camping in nature and cities are uniquely different, I've learned to prioritize environments where I feel safe enough to feel comfortable, day or night.

REALITIES OF THE ROAD

Vanlife is not monochromatic. People in this lifestyle are incredibly diverse and navigate various intersections (socioeconomic, cultural, and racial identities, just to name a few), which are significant contributors to the level of comfort and ease one may experience within road travel and outdoor spaces. Each of our experiences is unique and I can only speak to my own. I was curious to hear perspectives from other members of my community, so I shared an anonymous poll on social media asking two questions. The responses came from individuals who identify as BIPOC, trans, gender nonconforming, LGBTQIA+, disabled, solo women, and/or families.

1. What has made you feel unsafe on the road?

◎ Disgusted looks when I hop out in the morning with my dog. "Don't mind me, I'm just queer and homeless."

◎ Having to use men's restroom/showers when there are no unisex or single-stall options.

◎ Police make me feel unsafe.

◎ Being Black and in unknown territories and stopping at gas stations in small towns.

◎ When my campground neighbor flies a confederate flag.

◎ Towns and cities where I stand out from the rest of the demographic.

2. What tools have you implemented to protect yourself and your sense of safety on the road?

◎ Life360 location tracker app with family.

◎ Planning where we park and sleep and having two different spots we've scoped out, just in case.

- A safety plan and always backing in, so we're able to exit quickly.

- Safety check: make sure all my fluids, tires, door locks, and lights are working, and I make sure I can see a clear view around.

- Camping on designated land only. Trusting our instincts.

- Never riding with under a quarter tank of gas, that way I can keep going to the next station if the first one's sketchy.

- I took a self-defense course. I lie about my trip when strangers ask too many questions that make me uncomfortable, and I don't post my trip on social media until it's over.

There are some realities of the road that I'll never get used to. Waking up in the middle of the night to a *thump thump thump* on the window is jarring. It wasn't long into our travels when Dustin and I first got the dreaded knock. We were just outside of a small Virginia town, en route to Shenandoah National Park. It was well after dark when we decided to stop for the night, and for lack of a better option, we found a wide pullout on a rural road. Back then, the urge to see and do it all was still fresh in our minds, so we often found ourselves driving past dusk. It was around two in the morning when the police officer roused us from our slumber and ordered us out of the van. We scrambled in the dark for our clothes, threw on the first things we could find, and stepped outside, Dustin in his boxers and me wearing his T-shirt and sweatpants. I remember squinting at the sharp beam from the flashlight in my face and the train of questions that followed: "Where are you coming from? Where are you going? Why are you sleeping in your vehicle?" A wave of shame washed over me on the heels of his last question. I heard my voice tremble as I attempted to rationalize our motives and circumstance, but nothing made sense. "We're traveling," Dustin interjected, "we just needed a place to park for the night." For what seemed like hours, I stood tense and speechless, my heart pounding, while the officer ran our information and continued to interrogate us—he just couldn't wrap his head around the idea that we lived in our van. He finally said, "Well, you can't stay here, this is a respectable neighborhood." That was all I needed to hear;

within minutes Irie's pop top pulled shut and her wheels sped off into the night.

That was the first of several interactions we've had with police since beginning to live on the road. No matter how many times it happens, it never feels normal. Flashing blue lights pulling up behind us or that hard, urgent knock on our van in the middle of the night still make my stomach sink. I've chosen never to step outside or answer a knock on my van unless I absolutely must. Dustin acts as a buffer in each encounter, quickly stepping out and closing the door behind him. But we're never dishonest with the authorities; when asked, he lets them know I'm in the van. Sometimes they'll call out to me for due diligence, but I've never been required to step out, which is fine by me. Standing in a place of relative safety behind Dustin's white male privilege is something I do not take for granted in situations like these on the road.

Despite this buffer, I've come to accept that the dreaded knock is inevitable for those of us living vanlife. For me, and many other BIPOC, it's one of the biggest concerns we have in living on the road. But it's not the only one. Whether you're a full-timer, weekend warrior, or anything in between, road travel comes with inherent risks. And while they're all valid, they should not prevent you from pursuing your dream of vanlife and travel or opening yourself up to new experiences on the road. With some planning and precautionary measures, it is possible to minimize potentially unsafe situations and be prepared for when they do arise. Use the tips below as a guide to help you stay safe on the road.

HOW TO INTERACT WITH AUTHORITIES

Preparation:

Ensure that your driver's license, vehicle registration, and insurance are always up to date and on your person or in your rig. If you store your documents electronically, keep additional paper copies so you don't have to hand your phone to the officer.

If you're pulled over or questioned (this applies if you're driving or if you're camping and get the knock):

- Remain calm, keep your hands on the wheel or in sight, and avoid sudden movements.

- Provide your license, registration, and insurance upon request and always let the officer know if you're going to reach for anything.

- If you're asked to step out of the vehicle, do so calmly with your hands in sight.

- Do not argue with or disrespect the officer.

- If you're given a ticket, sign it and ask if you're free to leave. You can always dispute the ticket in court if you choose. The point is, don't make it an issue with the officer, you could be arrested for refusing to sign a ticket.

- If you are arrested, comply with the officers. Do not resist arrest.

Know your rights:

- You have the right to remain silent. Simply say, "I want to remain silent."

- You have the right to refuse a search; however, never physically resist a search. Say, "I do not consent to a search."

- You have the right to know what you're being stopped or questioned for. Ask, "Am I free to go?" If they say yes, leave calmly. If they say no, ask, "Can you tell me why you're stopping me?"

- You have the right to record an interaction with police but do so with discretion. If you're traveling with a partner, make sure one of you is recording the interaction. If you're alone, you can set your phone or camera on the dash to record or call someone you trust and have them listen in.

- If you are arrested, you have the right to an attorney. Say "I'm exercising my right to remain silent" and "I want to speak to an attorney."

Proactive Vehicle Maintenance

Perform a visual check of your rig daily or before leaving camp—inspect your tires and check tire pressure, check oil and coolant levels.

Go deeper on monthly checkups and before driving long distances—inspect belts, hoses, air filter, battery connections, windshield wipers, exterior lights, brakes, and tires. Be diligent and address any issues that arise.

Schedule a full vehicle inspection every three to five thousand miles, or three to six months. Do a walk-through with the mechanic. Have them change the oil and filter, rotate the tires, and inspect everything from your monthly checkup list. Address any issues per the mechanic's recommendations. As they say, an ounce of prevention is worth a pound of cure.

Planning Your Travels

Map out your route in advance to help avoid unforeseen circumstances, and have an alternate route as a backup. I like to plan essential stops such as fuel and estimate the time and mileage to my destination.

Check the weather forecast in the region(s) you're traveling through, as some places are more unpredictable than others. Stay up to date to prevent potentially dangerous situations.

Share your travel plans with someone you trust, especially if you'll be off-grid. Let them know where you're going and an estimated date you'll be back in service. When you return, check in.

Top up your fuel when the needle drops below half a tank. I get nervous when Irie is near a quarter tank, especially on long stretches of lonely highways. I recommend always having a gas can with extra fuel.

Research the places you're camping and recreating and follow all rules and guidelines, especially when it comes to wildlife and fire safety. Do not trespass on private property.

Accidents and breakdowns happen, and always at the most inconvenient times. That's one reason we avoid night driving nowadays, since it increases the risk of accidents, especially on dark, rural highways. Keep a roadside tool kit in your rig and make sure your spare tire and jack are in good working order and that you know how to use them. Have a basic understanding of your vehicle's mechanics (see Appendix A for more on this important topic). It's also a good idea to subscribe to a roadside assistance service; Dustin and I are longtime AAA Premier members.

CHAPTER 8

Routine in an Unconventional Life

Beep. Beep. Beep.
I'd roll out of bed to the
clamor of my alarm clock
and launch into my day
with the muffled sounds of
New Orleans waking up
outside my window.

Put on the kettle, take a quick shower, brush my teeth, make coffee, grab my prepacked breakfast/lunch from the fridge, jump in my car, turn on NPR, merge into traffic on the highway, and drive an hour to work. All before six a.m.

After a long day of work, I'd commute two hours back home, stuck in traffic more often than not. Then I'd go for a run if I had spare energy, take a shower, prepare dinner, pack my breakfast/lunch for the next day, do the dishes, and finally collapse on the couch in front of the TV. I was in bed by ten, set my alarm for the next morning, rinse, and repeat.

This was my pre-vanlife routine, done in the same order almost every day for years. I was good at it too; I would flow seamlessly from one activity to the next, with little thought involved. My routines kept me efficient, powered my produc-

tivity, and brought structure to my otherwise messy and chaotic daily life. And while these chores were necessary to get me from point A to B, I don't think I ever woke up actually excited for my morning routine.

I so desperately hoped vanlife would be different. Without the pressure of a nine-to-five work schedule, I would have all the time in the world to carefully craft and enjoy my days. I fantasized that I'd practice yoga every morning, boost my running endurance, prepare healthy meals, journal, and meditate. And I tried. My first year on the road I would wake up every morning and go through the motions of starting my day much like I did before. But, as I quickly learned, everything takes longer when you live in a van. And no matter how I tried, I couldn't seem to find a rhythm or make any kind of routine stick. Each morning was different from the next. The inconsistency was destabilizing and, at times, left me feeling hopeless.

As we know, vanlife is an unpredictable lifestyle. In fact, change is often the only constant. Since no two days are the same, sticking to a consistent routine is a challenge. If you're like Dustin and me, you either spend your days chasing adventure, running errands in a city, or hunting down Wi-Fi for work. All that can happen only when you're not driving long distances to get to your next location. This makes developing and maintaining a routine on the road much different than in a stationary lifestyle. The comfort of waking up in a home that's in the same place every day, stepping outside into a familiar neighborhood, and having a consistent schedule make it easy to go through the motions of daily routines. As does having all the conveniences of a stationary home, like a full-size kitchen, a bathroom and shower, and extra square footage to move freely—which are all things that don't typically fit in a van. Simply put, we cannot bring the complicated habits of our stationary lives into vanlife.

Routines fail in vanlife when:
- We're in a mindset of "see and do it all."
- We're not honoring our mental and physical needs.
- We seek perfectionism; we try to be perfect or make everything around us perfect.
- We're too rigid with our expectations and schedule.
- We're unwilling to shift away from the "nine-to-five workday" model.
- They become redundant and boring in a lifestyle that is anything but.
- We struggle to adapt to inconsistency and ever-changing environments.
- Unexpected occurrences like breakdowns happen.
- We overcomplicate our goals.
- We're not intentional in the mundane, day-to-day tasks.

SIMPLIFYING HABITS & TURNING ROUTINES INTO RITUALS

One of the many reasons to choose vanlife is to live a less complicated life. Just as this lifestyle influenced my journey to minimalism, the same can be said about the routines and habits I brought with me.

The common theme is *simplify*. Develop tools that allow you to approach your day-to-day with ease, to know what you need to do and how you need to do it. I've found that by adopting a simpler approach to activities, chores, and tasks, I'm much more motivated throughout my day. Don't get me wrong—there are days when having two humans and a full-grown German Shepherd in an eighty-square-foot van still feels overwhelming and claustrophobic, but I've learned that by having fewer moving parts to our routines, and tools that enhance rather than make our vanlife harder, it's easier to make healthy habits stick.

For me, a simple routine is one that can be performed anywhere, in any climate, weather, terrain, or time zone.

Tips to Simplify Your Routine

◉ Follow the same holistic approach to redefining minimalism that I introduced in Chapter 4.

◉ Analyze the practices that you utilize in your day-to-day life, be it a morning routine, exercise, or self-care, and break them down to the essentials. Take a "quality over quantity" approach, keeping the items or practices that are most beneficial and releasing the rest.

◉ Reflect on what works for you and what doesn't and adjust until it fits with your natural rhythm.

In the same way that minimalism helped me create space for myself in the van, simplifying habits helped me to build routines that I actually enjoy and have been able to stick to on the road. But when I say "routine," I don't mean it in a traditional sense. Because the traditional idea of routine is not well-suited for vanlife. Here's why:

Routines are a means to an end, a way to streamline and essentially automate the mundane and tedious parts of our day, thus reserving our mental energy for the parts that society deems important: that is, where we can maximize our productivity. Routine can take intention out of our actions and in vanlife, lack of intentionality can leave even the smallest task messy and complicated.

I know this sounds like a contradiction. How the hell can I expect you to create routines that stick while also telling you that routines don't work in vanlife? The answer is all about mindset. I've found that by moving away from a mindset of "routine for the sake of productivity," and instead applying mindfulness to my daily tasks, I've been able to adapt tools and create rituals that bring joy and meaning into my life. For example, developing and maintaining a vanlife workout routine was always a priority for me, but it wasn't something I enjoyed. It always felt like a chore. Still, I set high expectations for myself—I needed to run five miles or complete an hour yoga session to feel a sense of accomplishment. And when I fell short of these goals, I felt like a failure, which made it even harder to try again the next day. Any setback (of which there can be many in vanlife) became a reason to skip my workout—bad weather, a late

night at the campfire, waking up in a Walmart parking lot—and my progress toward making it a habit would be lost. When I shifted my mindset from routine to ritual and brought mindfulness to each and every workout, I learned to enjoy the process. In my practice of running, I focus my attention on where it's most needed in my body, my lungs expanding and contracting with each breath, the impact of my feet on the earth, the sensation of the wind on my face. Running in different environments and varying seasons has given me a new way to experience the world

lease it. As a yoga instructor, I've come to embrace intuitive movement as essential for health and wellness. Your body knows what it needs, so tune into that. It may not always be comfortable, but it will be beneficial. And using the term "movement" to describe my self-care ritual for physical and mental well-being frees me to be more authentic in my physical activities. I choose what brings me joy and makes me feel restored in mind and body.

In addition to elevating my physical health, regular physical activity grounds me and it's one of my finest tools for giving extra love to my mental well-being. I've spoken to many vanlifers who agree that exercise is one of the most challenging routines to create and maintain while on the road. When traveling from one place to the next, it's easy to trick our brains into thinking we've been physically active. When my butt's in a seat all day, whether driving or riding, the last thing I want to do at the end of the day is run five miles or do fifty push-ups. But it really doesn't need to be a big commitment. Just keep things simple: I enjoy hiking, playing with my dog, tossing a frisbee, Hula-Hooping, jumping rope, stretching, ice-cold swims, cleaning and downsizing my van, or cooking a healthy meal. In 2020, one thing that got me through some of the loneliest and most challenging times was solo desert dance parties. Yeah, I did that. I danced alone, barefoot under the stars to soca and calypso music from Trinidad. I cried and sang at the top of my lungs. I exhaled, released, reconnected, and refilled my cup. Don't underestimate the power of a good twerk sesh. Ya heard it here first, y'all!

as I travel and deepened my appreciation for the places I visit. I've come to view my physical rituals in a holistic way, which has trickled into all aspects of my life on the road. And while I still love running first thing in the morning, I don't beat myself up when it doesn't happen.

I've learned that there is no blueprint for vanlife, that each experience is different and most of us are making it up as we go. It's helpful to be flexible and remain open to reimagining old ways of thinking. The words we use matter, so if the term "exercise" brings up negative feelings for you, re-

> **TOOLS FOR CREATING MOVEMENT RITUALS FOR PHYSICAL & MENTAL WELL-BEING**
>
> ◉ Release the idea of "routine" in the traditional sense and focus on developing rituals as an embodied experience.
>
> ◉ Start creating your movement rituals before you move into your van and simplify your practice.
>
> ◉ Assemble your vanlife movement arsenal with practical, multiuse tools and equipment.
>
> ◉ Make time in your day to move your body, even if that means a simple stretching session or going for a walk.

PRIORITIZING SELF-CARE AS A RADICAL ACT

The events of 2020 greatly impacted all of us and changed the world as we know it. Managing the grief and loss of the coronavirus pandemic; the racial uprising that followed the murders of Ahmaud Arbery and George Floyd and the killing of Breonna Taylor; unemployment; police brutality; civil unrest; the economy; and an election that seemed to go on forever had many people feeling like they were hanging on by a thread.

Living in a van on the road as a Black-identifying woman, even in "normal" times, I've struggled with the shame, guilt, and anxiety that stem from stereotypes and societal expectations. And in a lifestyle that can already be lonely, the pandemic brought on a new level of tremendous isolation for me. Experiencing the myriad of racial traumas that took center stage—Black bodies murdered at the hands of the police, Black Lives Matter demonstrators vilified and brutalized, Black and brown communities disproportionately affected by COVID-19—left me navigating in a constant state of hypervigilance and, at times, fear.

Living vanlife doesn't make us immune to the world's struggles, even though sometimes it may seem like we're insulated from the ills of society. Nor does vanlife eliminate our personal baggage. In choosing to live this lifestyle, we bring our biases and baggage with us on the road. Combine that with the stresses of travel, inconsistent routine, unpredictability, and uncertainty, and self-care can often take a back seat.

Caring for myself is not self-indulgence,
it is self-preservation, and that is an act
of political warfare.

—From *A Burst of Light and Other Essays*
  by Audre Lorde

I've never been very good at prioritizing my own self-care. Culturally, it's not something I was raised with. Growing up I was taught that the needs of women were secondary to those of men. In BIPOC communities like mine, women are expected to be the strength and pillar of their families, holding everything together while de-prioritizing their own needs. As a child, I watched my mother work herself ragged, putting the needs of my father and brothers above her own until she was too sick and too tired to get out of bed. As a young girl, I was expected to do the same, so I brought this mindset with me into my adult life and vanlife.

The first time I was exposed to the concept of self-care, I was a couple of years into vanlife. Initially, I thought it meant enjoying a glass of wine in a bubble bath and getting weekly massages—good things, to be sure—but when I stumbled upon this powerful quote by Audre Lorde, it triggered a new perspective. It encouraged me to explore the idea of self-care as a radical act. I'm not exaggerating when I say it's been life changing. I'm empowered to prioritize my needs, recognizing that my self-care is not only essential but something I deserve. And from where I'm standing, that's revolutionary.

If you're already living vanlife, you know that prioritizing self-care in this lifestyle is easier said than done. As a digital nomad and remote entrepreneur, I often find myself slipping back into the grind culture, sitting in front of my computer for hours and days on end, not taking breaks, not eating properly or hydrating, prioritizing productivity over self-care, and experiencing burnout. In these moments, recalling the words of Audrey Lorde reminds me that radical self-care means challenging society's conditioning when it comes to my well-being. It means saying no and setting boundaries, even if I must set boundaries with myself, because you can't pour from an empty cup. For me, it's a generational shift, taking back my power, especially as a woman of color. It's a process of unlearning and relearning self-preservation. Radical self-care is not only essential but also vital to our collective healing.

AN ODE TO REST

I have a romantic relationship with Rest. Every day around 2:00 p.m. we meet for a date. Sometimes on my mat in the park, on the trail, in my hammock under a shady tree, or in my van for tea. We connect, observe, breathe. I always walk away feeling restored. When I was a child, our budding romance was forbidden, deemed lazy and indolent, but deep down I knew Rest could liberate me. There have been times as an adult where I've taken Rest for granted. In college, we were on-again, off-again. When I entered the corporate world, we almost lost touch completely—the grind got the best of me. Days, months, years went by, but I never forgot about Rest. In vanlife, we've rekindled our old flame. Meticulously, gently, boldly. Me and Rest, we're reclaiming my time and healing my spirit.

When I left New Orleans in 2016, I was an anxious little bird with a broken spirit, exhausted and traumatized. For many years I gave away pieces of my soul to the corporate world in exchange for tokens to continue playing the capitalist game. In my first few months on the road, sleeplessness was an issue for me, and this was partially tied to my sense of safety, or lack

> Rest is not some cute little luxury item you grant yourself as an extra treat after you've worked like a machine and are now burned-out. Rest is our path to liberation, a portal for healing, a human right.
>
> —The Nap Ministry, founded 2016

thereof. But really, how many of us get enough sleep? [**Puts hand down awkwardly.**] I don't think I know anyone in vanlife who can say they consistently get enough quality sleep. If we are to sustain ourselves in this lifestyle, we must slow down enough to create rituals of resting centered around mental health and well-being. How else can we heal from our traumas, deconstruct white supremacy, and reimagine a liberated world if we are not getting the thing that is most crucial to healing our bodies and minds?

Throughout my time on the road, I've explored many forms of rest as part of my self-care and healing practices—going for walks, journaling, breathwork, self-massage, restorative yoga, sitting in nature, meditating, cuddling with my partner or dog, and taking intentional breaks from technology and social media. On my path to healing, centering rest has deepened my commitment to self-love and helped me to recognize the destructive and oppressive systems that I had bought into. Now there are few things more essential to my self-care than rest.

So, in the words of the Nap Bishop, Tricia Hersey, "Lay yo ass down!"

Tools for Prioritizing Self-Care on the Road

- Embrace rest in all its forms.

- Note the areas in which you're doing a good job at practicing self-care and the tools and strategies that are helping you in these areas.

- Examine areas where you're struggling with self-care and where you're not prioritizing the things that are important to you.

- Create a plan for prioritizing self-care in areas where you're falling short.

- Pick one area around which to create and implement a self-care strategy.

- Incorporate pre-bedtime rituals such as meditating, stretching, or journaling.

- Schedule naps into your day and set bedtime reminders to ensure you get a proper amount of sleep.

- Tune into your mind and body and listen to what it needs. Sometimes that may mean taking a break from the road, whether that's staying with a friend or family member, or getting a hotel or Airbnb.

- Give yourself grace if you fall short.

My vanlife story is gritty and messy, filled with many breakdowns, challenges, and changes. The journey has been a balancing act of surrender and acceptance, ebbing and flowing with the seasons. Early on, I had no clue what I was looking for, all I knew was that I needed to make a change. Don't get me wrong—some days I'm still wondering what the hell I'm doing with my life, but I've learned that you don't have to know what you're looking for in order to find what you need.

Bottom line: mindfulness adds meaning and intention to our daily tasks, no matter what lifestyle we live. By simplifying our habits and creating rituals in lieu of routines, we can prioritize self-care and adopt tools to enhance our mental, physical, and spiritual well-being on the road. Think of it this way: if mental health is the road, then self-care is the vehicle.

CHAPTER 9

How to Make Money on the Road

A sea of chalk-white salt stretches as far as the eye can see, shimmering as the sun crests over the mountains behind me. The silhouettes of surrounding peaks and valleys bloom into vibrant hues of copper, red, and gold.

This is Badwater Basin, Death Valley National Park, California—the lowest point of elevation in North America. It's also my office location for the day.

I've positioned Irie at a good vantage point, allowing me to take in the view through the open sliding door. As I sit in quiet contemplation, alternately admiring nature's impressive display and typing my notes for this chapter, several passersby work up the nerve to approach. I know their questions even before they ask them. *"Beautiful van; what year is it?"* *"Is this a four-wheel drive?"* *"Does it have a bathroom?"* These are just pleasantries leading up to the most common question I receive from interested strangers and vanlife-curious folks: *"How do you make money while living and traveling in a van?"*

When Dustin and I first decided to pursue vanlife, we had no idea what we would do for money. We had saved a little before embarking, though not nearly enough to last an entire year.

But we pride ourselves on being resourceful, so I was confident we'd figure it out and we did. So now when people ask us what we do for a living or how we sustain ourselves on the road, I always grin a little. Why? Because the answer is far from straightforward.

Our initial plan wasn't to permanently move our lives onto the road. It was a one-year road trip from New Orleans to Alaska and back again. We had planned to go slow, live frugally, and figure out ways to keep the dream alive. But two weeks before we were scheduled to hit the road, something unexpected—but good—happened. Dustin gave his resignation at work and his boss responded by asking him to stay on part-time in a remote capacity until he could find a replacement. We were floored! Even though it was temporary, this meant we could take our time and not have to worry about finding work right away. Instead, we could focus on getting our feet, or our wheels, under us in our new journey.

One of the things that makes vanlife so appealing and has made it possible for us to keep going in this lifestyle is that it comes with low overhead—no rent or mortgage, no utility bills, and relatively few opportunities for impulse buys. Our biggest expenses are food and fuel. For the first year on the road, we lived on a budget of less than $1,800 per month. This low cost of living meant we didn't need to work forty-plus hours per week to make ends meet. The combination of low overhead and more free time gave me the ability to explore and develop passions that had taken a back seat until then. My writing and photography, which started out as a fun hobby, grew into a side hustle and, eventually, a business (more on that later).

Since trading my New Orleans apartment for a home-on-wheels, I've dabbled in many pecuniary endeavors and come up with some creative ways to make money on the road, some more exciting than others. My favorite, by far, was a fall season working on a cannabis farm with a group of vanlife OGs and an eclectic mix of immigrants. Together, we all fit under the umbrella term "modern nomad." We were American vanlifers and global travelers from Israel, Mexico, Italy, Brazil, the Czech Republic, all planting temporary roots, with the same goal of making money to fund the next leg of our wanderings. I'd be remiss if I didn't mention that, among this diverse group of misfits, for the first time in a long time, I wasn't an "only"—the only BIPOC or the only immigrant.

Farm work was physically demanding—sunrise to sunset, harvesting, drying, trimming.

But thanks to our transient microcommunity, it was also an immensely enriching and memorable experience. Communal dinners of nourishing ethnic cuisines with fresh ingredients from our home-grown garden—Mexican mole, homemade Israeli flatbreads and *bureka* (a pastry of potatoes, mushrooms, and cheese), New Orleans gumbo, and, of course, my Trini curry. We'd trade stories of our travels around nightly campfires, sing and dance, then at sunrise share a dense breakfast of porridge and coffee on the back porch before heading out to the fields. On any given day, there were gifts of yoga, Reiki, and other wellness rituals, Brazilian capoeira classes, and archery lessons.

Life on the farm was never dull. Even though I was perpetually exhausted and dirty, it was probably the only time on the road where I felt like I had a proper work-life balance. It also opened me up to a way of being that I had only ever experienced at my grandmother's house as a child—communal living. There was so much about it that just made sense. That fall in the beautiful foothills of California's Sierra Nevada mountains, a group of strangers and I became family. We worked hard, made money, and watched the fall foliage of the quaking aspen trees transform to vibrant yellows, oranges, and reds. By the time they shed their leaves, we had all parted ways and were off to our next adventures.

Other jobs were less thrilling. Like the time someone recommended filling out online surveys for extra cash. I figured I'd try it, what did I have to lose? Life on the road is about staying open, after all. Well, my dream of financial freedom through online surveys was short-lived. After I received a check in the mail for fifteen cents, I decided my time would be better served trying something a bit more lucrative.

Some gigs happened by accident. On our way to Great Sand Dunes National Park and Preserve, an electrical malfunction put Irie's house battery out of commission. So, in the quaint mountain town of Westcliffe, Colorado, we stopped at a bar and grill to charge our phones and grab a quick lunch. Five hours and a bar full of friends later, I ended up with a two-week waitressing gig, which led to Dustin and me selling crafts at the local farmers' market. We earned some quick cash, fixed Irie's electrical issues, and refilled our cups.

But the types of work that have been most fulfilling and financially rewarding for me—writing, storytelling, and photography—started as hobbies. Shortly before getting on the road, I started the @irietoaurora Instagram account as a fun place to provide updates from my travels. Sharing snippets from my life on the road ignited an interest in photography and led me to rediscover the love for storytelling that my grandmother had nurtured in me as a child. I couldn't afford a camera, so I settled for a cheap lens adapter for my iPhone. Eventually, I saved up for a DSLR and my hobby turned into a full-blown passion. I took some free online photography courses to help develop my skills. I never stopped writing and sharing, even when it was bad; I stayed true to myself and did my best to remain authentic.

Over time, @irietoaurora evolved into a space where I could experiment with these growing passions. I was able to build a solid network of supporters, mentors, friends, and a beautiful community that I'm ever grateful for. Through social media networking, I started writing articles and selling photography for brand websites and travel blogs. I didn't make much money at first, but it was enough to motivate me to continue pursuing these passions. It was a long game that I could never have imagined leading to me writing a book. And there were learning curves, to be sure. I cringe sometimes looking back on some of those early writings and photos—poor grammar, oversaturated skies. But that vulnerability and determination led to opportunities for me to turn those passions into a business. Now I'm proud to say that I'm a six-figure remote entrepreneur since 2021.

If there's one thing I hope you take away from this, it's don't be afraid to try new things. It doesn't have to be writing or photography; maybe you're interested in cooking, or painting, or fitness. You could start a YouTube channel giving cooking lessons from your van, sell your artwork at farmers' markets, vanlife gatherings, or other events, be a fitness consultant or online trainer. Vanlife presents an opportunity to connect deeper with the things that bring us the most joy and channel them into lucrative sources of revenue. There's no doubt that writing and photography are my passions, but I've also worked on a few startups, toyed with arts and crafts, and engaged in intentional community building, among other things. All of which have contributed to my life as a digital nomad and remote entrepreneur.

THE RISE OF REMOTE WORK

Before Dustin's fortunate parlay of a remote job, I had only ever known one other person who worked remotely. This was not long after I moved to the US, and I remember being fascinated by the concept of working from home—more time in the morning, not having a daily commute, and managing my own schedule. But it also seemed like an unattainable dream for someone like me.

Fast-forward twelve years. My decision to live vanlife opened me up to new possibilities, but early on, remote jobs were still relatively uncommon. The emergence of freelance websites like Upwork and FlexJobs created opportunities for self-employment and, for most of our time on the road, Dustin has maintained a consistent income from freelancing through these sites. Simultaneously, the advancements of off-grid technology—affordable solar equipment, mobile hotspots, Starlink satellite internet—have made it easier to work from the road and in remote locations. This confluence of conditions, along with the growing popularity of #vanlife, brought about a new type of traveling professional I like to call the overland digital nomad.

SEASONAL WORK

Farming: Examples include harvesting peaches in Colorado, the sugar beet harvest in the Midwest, and cannabis farms in California. Websites like wwoof.net and growfood.org connect travelers with opportunities for seasonal farmwork.

National parks: Summer is the busiest time in America's national parks, creating opportunities to volunteer with the Park Service or find service industry jobs in the parks' restaurants, hotels, and campgrounds.

Ski resorts: If snow sports are your passion, you can have it all during ski season. Every winter, ski resorts and ski towns across the country hire seasonal workers to fill a variety of jobs created by the influx of tourists—ski instructors, hotel staff, food service, guides, maintenance persons, and more.

Commercial fishing: Positions include deckhand on fishing boats, processing, and diving in areas ranging from trawling, crabbing, and harvesting shellfish. Seasons vary depending on the location.

Adventure guide/instructor: If you're skilled and passionate in a particular area of outdoor adventure, guide/instructor opportunities include leading rafting and kayaking, rock climbing, mountain biking excursions, glacier tours, and more. Many of these jobs include lodging, food, and training.

Lifeguard: Employed during summer months, lifeguards and swim instructors work in aquatic centers, at youth summer camps, and on public beaches.

Outdoor youth mentor: This could be at summer camps or through an organization, as a field mentor or counselor leading outdoor excursions, teaching new skills, and creating meaningful and transformational outdoor experiences for youth.

Overland digital nomad, noun. Someone who uses technology to earn an income while traveling and working remotely from the road.

While all overland digital nomads work remotely, we typically fall into one or more of the following categories—remote employee, freelancer, or entrepreneur.

- **Remote employee:** a full- or part-time employee of an organization who works from home or from any remote location away from the company's office. Also referred to as a traditional employee or W-2 employee.

- **Freelancer:** a self-employed worker who typically works on a project-by-project basis and is responsible for their own taxes and insurance.

- **Entrepreneur:** a self-employed business owner.

On the road, Dustin and I have belonged in each of these categories at one time or another. Starting as a part-time remote employee, Dustin later leveraged his skills and experience from his remote job to transition to a self-employed freelancer, working with several companies on a project-by-project basis. This was a bold and courageous move that he debated for some time before cutting the cord from the traditional employer-employee relationship. In the process, he gave up job security and a guaranteed paycheck but gained more control over his career, how he used his time, and the projects he chose to work on. Eventually, it was less about working for a dollar and more about aligning with his values. Watching Dustin create his path and make it up as he went was empowering for me. And I'm proud of him for going after it, especially at a time in our lives when nothing was certain.

Things were different for me. I couldn't parlay my job as an environmental scientist into a remote position, so leaving my career for the unknown felt like jumping into the deep end with no floaties. This experience motivated me to pursue my dream of entrepreneurship. Since I no longer had a career path to follow, all options were on the table. I was starting with a clean slate and re-creating my life all over again. It was intimidating at first because I had no idea what it meant to be an entrepreneur and, to be honest, I'm still not sure of the exact definition; I'm making it up as I go. But I'm in control

of my path. It's hard at times, but if there's one thing I'm absolutely sure of, it's that this is the path for me. I have never felt more aligned with my truth.

Dustin and I blazed our own paths as overland digital nomads because there were few options out there when we got started. It was challenging and discouraging at times, and it required a lot of resourcefulness and creativity to figure it out. And even with the growing freelance market, remote work options were still scarce our first few years on the road. But the times they are a-changin' (cue Bob Dylan).

In early 2020, COVID-19 threw all our lives into uncertainty. Lockdowns and stay-at-home orders were implemented, unemployment skyrocketed, and the economy screeched to a halt. Like most folks, I was left wondering how I would continue to sustain myself without the work that I depended on. But, despite all the tragedies during the first year of the pandemic, something positive developed. Companies and organizations, faced with a workforce that couldn't come to work, had to find ways to bring the work to the workers. And thus, the *work-from-home revolution* was born; now remote job opportunities are more abundant than ever and many individuals who were previously tied to a location-dependent job are free to join the vanlife ranks.

SOME JOBS FOR OVERLAND DIGITAL NOMADS

- photographer
- videographer
- graphic designer
- computer programmer and web designer
- virtual assistant
- copywriter
- consultant
- blog writer
- social media influencer
- YouTuber
- social media manager

- digital marketer
- remote project manager
- accountant or bookkeeper
- customer service representative
- online teacher
- life coach
- telemedicine professional
- traveling nurse
- remote therapist
- freelance copy editor
- freelance proofreader

and many more.

PROS & CONS OF REMOTE WORK IN VANLIFE

The lifestyle of a full-time vanlife digital nomad is not for everyone. Stepping away from the structures and routines of a traditional job can be overwhelming. And the financial insecurities that come along with it can be stressful and discouraging. In many ways, embracing vanlife while pursuing a career on the road is equivalent to stepping into the unknown and starting your life from scratch. While the ability to work remotely in vanlife can provide an opportunity to create the life of your dreams, it's not without significant challenges.

Downsides of working remotely on the road:

- Stepping away from the corporate world can mean having to pay for your own health insurance and losing other benefits, like a 401(k).

- Leaving behind the nine-to-five can mean losing financial security.

- Being your own boss in a life of travel makes it difficult to find a work-life balance, creating a potential for burnout.

- A flexible schedule can make it difficult to establish a routine.

- Working on the road sometimes means setting up your office from a coffee shop or a library or camping in a Walmart parking lot because you need a good cell signal.

Difficulties notwithstanding, the privilege to live a life of travel is something I do not take for granted. Until recently that privilege was reserved for the wealthy. But the sacrifices and progress made by generations that came before me have made it possible for me to live this dream. I've

Benefits of working remotely on the road:

◎ In vanlife, my home is always with me. That, combined with the location independence of remote work, provides the ability to stay for as long as I want in any destination.

◎ The low overhead of vanlife provided the space to pursue my passions and start a business.

◎ As my own boss, I work on my own terms and create my own schedule.

◎ The flexibility of this lifestyle allows me to pursue any opportunity that may arise.

My intention with life on the road was always to blur the line between work and play, but early on I didn't see how this would be possible. Focusing on my passions enabled me to shift my perspective and reimagine what success means to me. Even though I work a lot now, most days it doesn't feel like work. Pursuing my passions gave me a reason to keep learning and exploring new things. It's helped me to connect with like-minded people and foster relationships I never would have otherwise. And it's given me meaningful structure in my life on the road. Not everyone can turn their passions into a career. But if you're pursuing vanlife, my advice is to dedicate time to what energizes you, follow your curiosity, and don't be afraid to experiment and take risks.

been able to turn my hobbies and passions into a business, create my own path to financial independence, and redefine what success and happiness look like for me. Previously, there wasn't space in my life to explore these possibilities. Vanlife provided the opportunity; the rest was up to me.

CHAPTER 10

Relationships, Intimacy & Co-Living in a Van

"Just say yes," Dustin exclaimed, his hand propped on a boulder for balance as he halfway lowered to one knee with a ring in his right hand.

It was late summer of 2013, and we were backpacking on the Appalachian Trail in Georgia for my birthday. His plan was to propose on the summit of Blood Mountain, but on day two of our trek, Dustin took a bad step and twisted his knee, bringing an end to our trip and thwarting his romantic plans. So with a heavy pack on my back and Dustin's arm draped over my shoulder, we slowly hiked down the mountain. It was around midday when the heat and humidity kicked in, so we made frequent stops in the shade to rest and hydrate. I stepped away to admire a patch of wildflowers and when I turned around, there he was, attempting to get down on his one good knee. With my eyes wide, I walked over to him and said yes as I helped him to his feet. Turns out, he had carried the ring in his pack for three days. I even slept on it in my makeshift pillow and didn't know. We celebrated with protein bars and a flask of Trini rum while we waited for the shuttle to arrive that would take us back to our car.

The following spring, we were married in Dustin's hometown of Lake Charles, Louisiana. When we said our I do's, the dream of vanlife I had shared with him three years prior was buried under the thrill of starting our newlywed life. Living together in New Orleans was exciting—we had our careers, active social lives, and a bustling city that kept us entertained. We also had our growing pains as a newly married couple. But nothing could have prepared us for being together twenty-four/seven in the high-stakes, high-stress situations that would come with living and traveling in a van.

HOW VANLIFE PREPARED US FOR THE PANDEMIC

We had no playbook for how to navigate the drastic shift in our relationship that came with living in Irie. To be honest, we hadn't considered what it would be like to spend all day, every day together without the distractions of work or social time with friends and family. I had thought a lot about how great it would be to spend more time with my love, but the distinction between "more time" and "full-time" was something I didn't anticipate. It wasn't until we were a few months into vanlife, butting heads and getting on each other's nerves, that we both began to wonder if our relationship would survive this "new normal."

The intimate, close quarters of vanlife exacerbated the day-to-day issues we faced as a couple—dividing chores, cooking, dishes, morning routines, not to mention the fact that everything takes longer when you live in a van. We didn't anticipate the challenges of living off-grid and the added stress it would bring to our relationship. The learning curve for conserving and sourcing resources only heightened our differences in conscientiousness. Living immersed in the elements while adapting to new hygiene habits, such as dirty feet in the bed or not showering every day, caused irritation and tension.

But the real test came as the dissimilarities between our personalities were magnified within Irie's eighty square feet. With nowhere to hide and no outlet to make those small, temporary escapes that tend to provide breathing room, we quickly discovered each other's hidden insecurities, triggers, and vulnerabilities. We had tapped into a new dimension of our relationship, and neither Dustin nor I was equipped with the tools or self-awareness to navigate this precarious time. I was terrified—it felt like we were hanging on by a thread. The daily arguments over the little things were mere symptoms of our deeper emotional struggles, like the identity crises we were both trying to manage from our major life transition.

We were charting this new course through murky waters and it was frustrating. In desperation, we sought refuge in familiar societal gender roles—Dustin relegated himself to mechanical tasks, retreating to Irie's engine compartment whenever we made camp, and I obsessed over making our van a home. He became avoidant and I unconsciously defaulted to the same self-protective behaviors I developed as a child—acting tough and pretending I had it all put together when I obviously did not. My body responded to the stress with mood swings, lack of sleep, fatigue, acne, and anxiety. Our tiny van became a battlefield and we were both spent from co-existing in constant survival mode. Communicating healthy boundaries was another soul-sucking chore and, to top it all off, we literally had no privacy.

How did we get to this? played on repeat in my mind, and most of all, *How the hell do we get out of it?* This was supposed to be our new beginning, a fresh start where we could reevaluate our priorities, our relationship goals, and our well-being. But we had brought the same conditionings and habits with us into this new life, a sign of how deeply ingrained they were. This emotional roller coaster went on for months and finally came to a head on the Fourth of July 2016.

SIGNS THAT YOU'RE APPROACHING BURNOUT AND NEED TO REEVALUATE

- Feeling tired, fatigued, and lethargic.
- Finding it difficult to concentrate, even on things you would normally enjoy.
- Loss of creativity, motivation, or purpose.
- Feeling anxious or overwhelmed by everyday tasks, and frequently procrastinating.
- Feeling moody, irritable, or impatient, and sometimes snapping at your partner or others.
- Not eating properly or forgetting to eat altogether.
- Just needing to get things done for the sake of making it through the day or week.
- Not having time for personal care.
- Difficulty falling asleep or staying asleep, even when you're tired.
- Feeling isolated, helpless, or depressed, and adopting a cynical or negative outlook.

Dustin and I were eager to get out of the van and let loose for the first time since leaving New Orleans, so we planned a fun-filled weekend of music, food, and dancing in Crested Butte. Set against the backdrop of Colorado's stunning Elk Mountains, this charming mountain town is an adventurer's utopia year-round. In the winter, it's a skier's paradise and when the snow melts, it reveals countless opportunities for hiking, climbing, and mountain biking. I had read online that Independence Day in Crested Butte is "the country's biggest small-town celebration." Every Fourth of July, the town comes alive with music in the park, sidewalk art markets, food vendors, games, and fireworks. It sounded exactly like the reset we both needed.

Early on the morning of the Fourth, we hit the town. There were people everywhere wearing patriotic gear and waving miniature American flags, Bruce Springsteen's "Born in the USA" blasting from the speakers at every other storefront on the main street. It was a picture-perfect American experience. We grabbed mimosas and joined some friends for the annual pancake breakfast, then took a stroll to admire some local arts and crafts before heading to the park for live music. It was shaping up to be a beautiful day. Dustin and I were both fully present and feeling like ourselves—at ease, happy, refreshed.

Later that evening we took a gondola up the mountain to the ski resort for dinner, a concert, and the grand finale Fourth of July fireworks show. Sitting in the grass with the colorful display overhead and Dustin's arms wrapped around me as I leaned back against him, we started talking about where we would camp for the night. I wanted to head out to some public lands nearby so we could sleep in and wake up slowly the next morning, but Dustin said he would rather stealth camp in town so we didn't have to drive in the dark. The back-and-forth escalated and tempers began to flare. The disagreement triggered anxieties and grievances that we had both been holding on to from the weeks and months prior. Unable to contain all the emotions, I stormed away with tear-filled eyes and left Dustin sitting in the grass.

Sobbing alone on the gondola ride down with all the dizzying thoughts in my head, I couldn't help but wonder if vanlife was a big mistake: it had destroyed my career, my self-esteem, and now my relationship. Back at the van, there was no sign of Dustin, so I locked the door and went to sleep. He showed up a few hours later, still upset, asking to

be let in, but I refused. The next morning, I woke up and found him sleeping in the passenger seat, having used the hidden key to get in. It wasn't my proudest moment.

Feelings of shame and guilt permeated the van. But for both of us, it was the question of "Is this the end of our relationship?" that really had us frightened. During that sad, sunny morning cooped up in the van, stealth camping on a resi-

the only factor—but it was the perfect storm that brought our issues into sharp focus. Of course we wanted to stay together, but our needs and desires were shifting as a couple and as individuals and this was something we needed to accept. It was the beginning of a challenging but important personal journey for both of us.

By the time we left that street corner in Crested Butte, we had reentered vanlife with a new lens. The pressures prompted us to think deeper about who we were and what we wanted out of this life. For me, that meant addressing the intergenerational traumas affecting my mental health and seeking professional help. This acceptance puts us in a very vulnerable place. For Dustin, it means continuously educating himself about the experiences I face as a woman of color navigating life on the road and learning to be more aware of our differences in privilege as an interracial couple.

Since then, we work every day to ensure that our van home is a safe space for healing and growth where we can both show up authentically. I'd be lying if I said it's been easy—the journey has tested us. And in the process, we've acquired tools that have strengthened us, both personally and relationally. We've learned to be more intuitive regarding each other's needs and developed communication styles that are validating, empathetic, and compassionate. We've learned how to be better listeners and how to support each other on our individual journeys. And, most important, we've worked to build a better relationship with ourselves.

dential street, we were forced to confront some hard truths about ourselves and our relationship. Everything was called into question: our communication styles, boundaries, emotional needs, goals, and ambitions. And the big question on the table was whether or not we would continue together in vanlife.

As much as I wanted to blame our new lifestyle for the hardships we were facing, vanlife wasn't

HOW TO KEEP THE LOVE ALIVE IN YOUR VAN HOME

SPEND TIME APART.

This can be hard to do in vanlife but it's important to carve out alone time. That could mean taking turns giving each other the van for a few hours by going for a walk or a hike or sitting quietly under a tree and journaling or listening to music. Dustin's an introvert and I'm an extrovert, so taking some solo time goes a long way in helping to recharge our batteries.

TRY NEW THINGS, TOGETHER & SEPARATELY.

Vanlife offers numerous opportunities to explore outside of your comfort zone, like picking up a new hobby or trying new activities together. In 2019, I traveled for a yoga teacher training retreat, leaving Dustin with the van for a month. The time apart was not only rejuvenating for us both but I also returned with the healing gift of yoga practice to incorporate into our life on the road. It's a bonding experience to share such a beautiful part of my heritage with Dustin.

CONTINUOUSLY WORK ON YOUR COMMUNICATION.

Healthy conversations take practice, so give yourselves grace, and don't expect perfection. For Dustin and me, it's helped to set ground rules before we address difficult and emotional topics. Living in a tiny, mobile space with another person requires good communication because things will regularly come up, whether it's "Can you move out of my way so I can change clothes?" or "Will you please wash that dish so we don't get flies?" or "I need some alone time." Communication is critical because it prevents issues from getting buried and festering. An important part of good communication is listening more.

ACKNOWLEDGE AND APPRECIATE.

In a close-quarters lifestyle like vanlife, it's easy to get consumed by the unpredictable and tedious minutiae—from breakdowns to organizational tasks and everyday chores, especially when you live, work, and play together. A willingness to validate your partner's efforts and personal growth is essential. Whether it's something big or small, showing gratitude is important. This is a way Dustin and I have continued to show appreciation for each other and strive toward our goals.

TAKE TIME OFF.

Life on the road can be stressful and exhausting, especially when cohabiting in a tiny space. Since our first year on the road, Dustin and I have prioritized taking time off the road whenever we need it. Whether that's getting a hotel room for a night with two beds so we can spread out, an Airbnb for the weekend, or even a rental for a month, it's been helpful in recharging and refilling our cups.

These tips have become mantras in our vanlife and were validated in 2020 when COVID-19 ushered in an unexpected and incredibly difficult relationship test. As lockdowns forced people to remain indoors, partners cohabiting found themselves living together twenty-four/seven. Fortunately, after nearly four years of sharing a tiny home on the road, Dustin and I felt equipped with the tools for managing many of the emotional, physical, and financial challenges that followed. It wasn't easy, but since we had already gone through the struggles of adapting to vanlife and working through the problems that arose, we were able to focus on the new issues we were facing, like keeping ourselves safe and healthy.

QUESTIONS TO ASK WHEN MOVING INTO A VAN WITH SOMEONE

There was so much that Dustin and I could not have foreseen even though we were already married and living together prior to moving into the van. We could not have anticipated how much we would change. But intentional and open communication can help to ease your transition into vanlife and help you to shift appropriately as things develop. The questions below are a good starting point to get ahead with important knowledge and help set you up for success in your relationship in vanlife. Let love and honesty be your guide.

- Do you consider yourself a morning person or a night person?
- What are your morning and nightly routines?
- Are there times when you are more sensitive to noise?
- Do you leave dishes in the sink or wash them immediately after use?
- How important is organization and cleanliness to you? Can you share examples of what that looks like to you?
- How important is alone time for you? How can we best communicate as those needs change?
- How do you feel about having guests in our van?
- What are your top goals or priorities for moving into a van?
- What is your argument style? Do you like to talk it out at once or take space?
- When disagreeing, how can we make sure we remain a team?
- What are your pet peeves?
- How will we divide bills, expenses, finances, etc.? Example: Share a bank account and/or credit card, take turns paying for every other tank of gas or grocery trip, split it at the pump or register, keep a tab and pay at the end of the week/month, etc.?
- How will we manage growth/changes that differ? Example: If vanlife is not working out for one of us, is maintaining a long-distance relationship an option?

—@queersextherapy, Instagram, and

@healingisimperfect, Instagram

ALTERNATE PERSPECTIVES

As I've said throughout this book, vanlife is not a one-size-fits-all lifestyle. There are many ways to live a life on the road and everyone's experience is unique. To offer different perspectives, I reached out to some vanlifers who come from diverse backgrounds and navigate vanlife in various living arrangements. Their advice and experiences are shared anonymously below.

How do you maintain romance and intimacy while living and traveling in a van with a partner or partners?

Travel can be tough on the body and the simplest tasks can take a lot of energy. Getting used to living on the road full-time was challenging for the first few months, so sexual intimacy wasn't always a priority. However, our emotional and mental intimacy really grew because we had to navigate a lot of challenging situations between van maintenance issues and being in a different environment regularly. Additionally, as an interracial and queer couple having to prioritize our safety in a different way, that shared experience grew our sense of intimacy as well. In general, just remind yourself that physical intimacy can come in cycles and it's okay for things to ebb and flow. That's important to remember if you're living life on the road with a partner(s). After we had some time to adjust to living in a tiny home, we found that being very intentional about creating space and time for romantic intimacy was the best way to maintain it. It can be really easy to deprioritize romance because so many other things are happening while living on the road, but we've found that taking advantage of little moments and intentionally creating space for romance is important. Also taking the pressure off of what "romance" should look or feel like allowed us to show up more for it because there was less stress around it. Although we haven't perfected this by any means, it has really helped us to be more intentional.

———————

I invested in this card game that you can play with your partner that asks thoughtful, conversation-provoking questions. It truly forces you to be 100 percent focused and present on what's currently taking place, nurturing that bond you have with each other. It allows for a channel of open communication whilst providing a space to have the difficult ones. It's been so incredible for intimacy and meaningful moments, especially when we spend so much time together in such a small space, it can be easy to take those for granted.

What are some of your biggest challenges living in a van with your partner(s) and how have you learned to deal with these challenges as your vanlife has evolved?

I think the biggest challenge is remembering that I'm no longer solo on the road, and that decisions are not just mine. It's no longer all about what I want to eat or where I want to go, and my rig is no longer my space alone. We've updated the space to support his needs and his belongings, and we've improved our communication. I also make sure he is involved in decisions to ensure that he has a hand on the steering wheel and is not just a passenger in our vanlife.

What are some of your biggest challenges when it comes to dating in vanlife and how have you learned to deal with them as your vanlife has evolved?

Constantly moving is the biggest issue. Individuals often are not okay with an open arrangement, or on the other end, with their partner traveling often/having to take space and be essentially long-distance. If I stay in one place for a while, after a few dates and trying to express to somebody that the rest of the year I'm traveling, they often don't fully grasp or accept that I really am out of state most of the time. How I've learned to deal with that . . . honesty, honesty, honesty. I've learned to have very clear communication, requests, boundaries, and understandings. I never hold back when communicating with a romantic partner about the realities of dating while traveling full-time. It can feel awkward sometimes, especially if somebody has only ever dated in a structured, monogamous, close-proximity relationship, but it is always worth it.

**How do you create and maintain personal space and autonomy
in your relationship in the van on the road?**

By respecting each other and what we as individuals value in our
"downtime." My partner loves to end his workdays by decompressing
and retreating into his thoughts for a few hours and getting lost in books.
I recognize when he is needing his personal space (or he'll vocalize his
feelings) and I'll occupy myself with my own hobbies. It's so important
that we don't just blend together into one thing. Having our individuality
is what attracts us to each other, so keeping that is the single most
important thing that we continue to maintain whilst living in such close
quarters. It's what makes the day-to-day interesting and different!

Learning to live outside your van when weather permits is a big one. When
I wake up, I open my van doors and they stay open for most of the day
until I go to sleep. This allows for your "space" to be much bigger than
the van. Taking time apart also means separate walks, catching up with
friends or family on phone calls, or going to a public library to work alone.

We allow each other to do something that brings us joy and the other
person will do their best to support that in whatever way it may look like.
We're strong believers in taking breaks from the road, such as spending
a couple of days in an Airbnb or at a hotel so that we can have a bit of
extra breathing room. Of course, this isn't an option for everyone, but it's
something we've always prioritized when setting our budget because it's
important to us. In general, we really believe in making sure we keep up
with our self-care, which usually includes working out, meditating, doing
yoga, journaling, going to AA meetings, and watching funny content.

We purchased a ten-by-ten-foot gazebo for additional outdoor shelter,
which allows me to do my work in a separate space from my partner.

TIPS FROM THE COMMUNITY

On navigating vanlife in a romantic relationship(s):

Remember that you're in this together. Make sure to listen to each other's needs, wants, etc. Share the responsibilities. My partner and I have always had rules like: if you cook, you don't wash the dishes that night, the other does. Also swapping and sharing the gross tasks (dumping our waste, cleaning the gray water tank tube, etc.) and trying to work together to get them done more quickly. It makes the mundane a bit more interesting.

On planning your days when cohabiting in a van:

Break up responsibilities and chores based on each person's situation. If I work remotely and my partner is unemployed, they often drive while I work in the front seat. This allows for us to use our time once we get to camp to truly focus on each other. Our "responsibilities" equal out, while our free time also equals out. Chores are split up based on preferences. I usually cook and they do the dishes. I do laundry and they fold. Communicating these needs and expectations up front also helps. So does checking in regularly to make sure the setup is working for everyone.

Tips and advice for dating in a van:

I've found that being open and honest about the realities of this lifestyle is very important. Many

people think of a solo vanlifer as just a transient unicorn that you see once and then never again. Sometimes this is the case, depending on the person. But if you're seeking more, or seeking less, it helps to know that [about yourself]. I would really recommend having a strong idea of what you're looking for, what you're open to, or even just knowing what you're not open to. For example, there was a time in my life when I was not interested in any exclusivity or relationship/ commitment. I was very fair with anybody I interacted with in the dating realm by letting them know up front. It's important for me to

the van is fun! You can park anywhere and get it on. A few tips we have for sex in a van are to make sure you have a safe and comfortable parking spot, make sure your parking brake is on, get some spicy or romantic lights, and find little ways to create spontaneity. So much of vanlife involves routine, and having too much "routine" around vanlife sex can take the fun and spontaneity out of it, so finding ways to maintain that will help.

———————————————

I personally can't have sex without having a shower prior or a solid "ho bath," so after my showers at the gym or out in nature, my partner knows he better get it while the getting is good (lol). And so what if it's a bus, it's my home. No parking lots; I need to be out in nature somewhere with no one near—a rocking bus is a dead giveaway for what's going on inside. Also the outdoor gazebo is a plus; it's like outside sex but you're not getting your ass eaten up by mosquitos.

protect myself and my feelings, wants, and needs but it's also important for me to be kind and respectful of others.

Tips for having sex in a van:
Everyone's needs, bodies, and preferences are different, so it's important to find what works for you as a couple. For us, we've always wanted our van to feel like home, so keeping our van clean and tidy has helped with having sex in the van. It's so easy to let things and chores pile up, but the more we stay on top of the cleanliness, the more we're comfortable having sex in the van. Having sex in

It's undeniable, when sharing space with another human(s) twenty-four/seven you have nowhere to hide your truest self. And being cooped up with partners and loved ones for extended periods will no doubt bring to light all our strengths and weaknesses. For Dustin and me, the first year of vanlife tested our relationship to the breaking point. But as we tried and failed and kept trying, we found ways to stay connected and support each other. Through it all, navigating the challenges of this lifestyle together has strengthened our relationship in ways we couldn't have imagined.

CHAPTER 11

Community & the Diversify Vanlife Movement

In the fall of 2016, Dustin and I were camped out on public lands somewhere outside of Yellowstone National Park.

It wasn't our best moment; we were cold, down-trodden, lonely, and silently wondering *What the heck are we doing with our lives?* We were nearing our six-month vanniversary and, as beautiful and exciting as the road had been up to this point, there was just something missing. That was, until I found myself lying in bed one morning scrolling through Instagram, huddled under several blankets while wearing nearly every piece of clothing I owned as I tried not to freeze. With one cold hand sticking out, holding my phone, I came across a shared post with the location and description of a van gathering in Bend, Oregon, taking place the following day. Almost instantly, I sprang up from under the blankets, shouting, "Dustin, there's a van gathering in Oregon! Let's go!" He didn't need convincing. Neither of us had ever heard of a van gathering, but the description—a meetup for humans who live in vans—was enough to fuel our imaginations. My stomach tightened and my head was spinning with equal parts nervousness and elation.

Bend was quite a haul from our current location in southern Wyoming, but we decided it was worth the drive—in less than half an hour, the van was packed and we were on our way. That may have been the first time that Dustin and I truly realized the power our lifestyle gave us, that our four wheels allowed us the freedom to move almost instantly, to leave if something wasn't working for us.

We answered this call of opportunity, and in pursuit of new experiences we drove all night and well into the morning. The trip to Bend was an estimated eleven-hour road trip, but our Irie likes to cruise at a snail's pace. We arrived in Deschutes National Forest the following afternoon and made our way down a dusty, jeep-rutted dirt road. A sense of excitement began to build as, through the dust, we spotted a tan Westy that looked just like our Irie, cartoonishly bouncing along ahead. Like Alice following the white rabbit, we followed it down the long, winding road, when suddenly the forest opened to a clearing.

Before us lay the most glorious, hodgepodge collection of vans we had ever seen. Here, beside a giant crater in the Oregon woods, we met road travelers from all walks of life—young, old, families, full- and part-timers, weekenders, and everything in between. That was the moment I realized what had been missing in our first six months of vanlife. That was when we found a community on the road.

The few early months of vanlife were some of the most challenging times of my life on the road. And even though I was traveling with a partner, it was still immensely lonely. After all, we were adapting to a new, unconventional way of living, a lifestyle that was still in its infancy. We didn't know anyone who was living even close to this way, much less who had quit their whole-ass career and sold all their personal belongings to pursue something they knew almost nothing about. Friends and family members alike were stunned at the decision. And I get it, we were supposed to be following the script—college, graduation, career, house, kids, retirement plan—but there we were, two lost thirtysomethings "ruining" our lives to live in an old van. It was hard to escape the noise and feelings of failure.

The most difficult part for me was overcoming the attachment with my identity away from my career. Initially being completely financially dependent on Dustin's remote work made me feel powerless. I've found that this is a feeling that's rarely talked about in the mainstream of vanlife, despite the fact that many people entering it experience grief from letting go. Our jobs

and careers are more than just the way we make a living and pay the bills—they give us structure, influence the way we see ourselves and others, and, believe it or not, have a huge impact on our sense of self-worth. Even though I wasn't in love with my pre-vanlife job, it still offered me a social outlet, gave me a reason to wake up every day, and provided me with meaning and structure. In vanlife, I was forced to rethink and rebuild that structure myself.

Remaking your life from scratch is no easy feat. When the message you receive from the world around you is that you're making a mistake, becoming a failure, or will never be able to return to society and a "real" job, you're left with feelings of shame and hopelessness. Even though life all around me was beautiful, my heart ached, and the loneliness and feelings of isolation were hard to overcome. The disconnect took a toll on my well-being and left me vulnerable.

That first vanlife gathering in Bend gave us reassurance and altered the trajectory of our journey, from a one-year road trip to full-on, full-time vanlife. We learned something from everyone—suggestions for organizing our tiny space, upgrades that would turn a van into a home, mechanical advice from other Westy-dwelling folks, camping and boondocking tips, and so much more. The ability to connect with and share in the experiences of other road travelers not only equipped us with an arsenal of tools that we would implement moving forward but also made us see this as a lifestyle we would sustain for as long as possible. *We could build a com-*

munity. Suddenly, I was hopeful again. Feelings of failure eventually dissipated as I redirected my energy into imagining new dreams, creating, connecting, networking, pursuing passions, learning new skills, and getting uncomfortable with new experiences. The lack of community was a void during those first six months on the road and finding it empowered me to push on in this lifestyle.

Through this culture of modern nomadism, we're reshaping the nature not only of how we live, work, and travel but of how we build community. Shifting away from the vacation model of travel changes the way we experience new places, people, and cultures. Rather than passing through like a tourist, the modern nomad is at home in all the places they visit, essentially becoming a short-term resident by shopping at the local grocery stores, dining in restaurants, working from coffee shops and libraries, effectively ingratiating themselves into the fabric of the community. And as the pandemic exposed cracks in society's foundation, forcing many to reassess their priorities, vanlife presented a viable alternative. This separation from a stationary way of living has necessitated a paradigm shift in the way we think about community, and social media has been instrumental in driving that change.

If you search #vanlife on social media, you'll find millions of posts—yes, millions. In the last few years, the vanlife community has grown exponentially, becoming one of the hottest lifestyle trends across the globe. This explosion can be

attributed, in large part, to social media. With platforms like Instagram, TikTok, and YouTube providing the opportunity for endless storytelling, how-to-vanlife blogs and videos, and picturesque images, vanlife has leapt into the mainstream. With a captive audience on social media, vandwellers have carved out space and inspired a generation by showcasing a different way of life, one that prioritizes ease, affordability, and the opportunity to live more authentically.

also given me an outlet for self-expression and creativity. But most important, it's helped me to discover social connection in a lifestyle that would otherwise be isolating, especially when living on the margins of society, and it's even helped me to find emotional support during tough times.

But in all honesty, my relationship with social media is complicated. At times, sharing snapshots of my story has made me vulnerable to trolls, inappropriate and offensive comments, and online harassment. It's also led me to prioritize online interaction over real-world relationships and has been a major trigger for anxiety and FOMO (especially during the pandemic when in-person interaction was limited). The social status that comes with having an online presence in our media-driven society has at times left me feeling a desperate need to create content for the consumption of others, which pulls me out of the present moment and leaves me living in an air of inauthenticity.

Although it is a mixed bag, I believe one of social media's most significant contributions to this lifestyle is the ability to galvanize and foster community. Social media is where I learned about my first vanlife gathering and where I first discovered the growing community of vandwellers through #vanlife. It's been the meeting place of the modern vanlife movement since its infancy and continues to be a place that facilitates connection in a way that helps this community to thrive—through collaborative and creative projects, networking, and job opportunities, especially in creative fields.

Social media has played a dynamic role in my life on the road. It's provided a platform through which I've rediscovered the power of my voice, it has influenced my career as a writer and photographer, and it's become an effective tool for my activism and advocacy work. Despite its addictive nature, social media has provided me with countless opportunities to find new friends and communities and network with new people who share similar interests and ambitions, and it's

RECOGNIZING THE NEED FOR CHANGE

In the summer of 2019, those virtual connections made on social media materialized into in-person meetups. It was the height of the vanlife movement and it seemed as if everyone was on the road, eager to explore, bond, and connect. Dustin and I were on a vanlife gathering circuit, traveling across the western US from Southern California to Idaho, Colorado, and New Mexico with a rotating caravan of nomads. Our calendar was filled with meetups, friend circles, and events. But as the summer wore on, it became difficult to ignore that at each of these events, I was typically one of the only BIPOC in a sea of white people. Almost universally, the stories and experiences shared were from a homogeneous perspective, further drowning out the voices of those with different and unique lived experiences. It was infuriating and demoralizing.

Sitting in a dusty dome in New Mexico at my third vanlife gathering of the season, I joined a group of fellow vandwellers for an organized community chat. This event is common at any vanlife gathering, along with community-led workshops and activities like yoga and meditation, journaling, and plein air painting, to name a few. The community chat is like a town hall forum, where members gather and, with the guidance of a facilitator, discuss shared subjects of interest and topics related to the well-being of the vanlife community—mental health, safety, sustaining vanlife, and more. The topic of discussion on that warm Saturday afternoon centered around vanliving and the narrative portrayed in the media.

As I've noted, one of the biggest pitfalls of #vanlife in the media is the romanticization of the lifestyle. This thread was woven throughout the conversation in the dome, with the consensus being that the media controls the narrative, while the individuals living this lifestyle are powerless to change it. But that notion is inherently false. Those of us who choose to live this lifestyle for the pleasure of travel carry a certain amount of privilege and we all play a role in the narrative being portrayed. And that is especially true for those with a platform and social following whose voices and images directly influence the narrative.

While the conversation in the dome that day touched upon the media's inaccurate portrayal of vanlife and its effects on the community, a crucial part was left out—that the false narrative signals to the world who is welcome in

the vanlife community and how vanlife is "supposed" to be. It creates barriers to entry for individuals who do not look like the "ideal vanlifer" or may not have the available resources or support to get started, and it ostracizes those who are forced into this lifestyle while leaving those navigating the margins vulnerable to stereotyping, tokenization, and violence.

I was mostly silent, as the conversation was dominated by two white-presenting men who shared their perspectives on "walking upright in the world" and "picking yourself up by your bootstraps." These privileged ideals silence and erase people with different experiences, people who come from different backgrounds and different circumstances, and people with disabilities who may find it difficult to "pick themselves up by their bootstraps." In the words of my dear friend Jayme Serbell, "It's hard to walk upright in the world when you've got oppression on your shoulders."

Walking out of the dome, I was overcome with a myriad of emotions—anger, sadness, isolation. A few friends followed me back to my van wearing the same look of exasperation. As we gathered around Irie with tears of frustration and a lot of cursing, we came to the realization that our community was divided. That was the moment I knew I could no longer stay silent.

REPRESENTATION MATTERS: A CATALYST FOR CHANGE

For several weeks I wrestled to process the incidents that took place that summer—the silencing, the tokenizing, the unsafe spaces that were being cultivated in my beloved community. I began to feel a steady buildup of isolation once again and considered removing myself from the community entirely. Deep down, I was longing for a space where I could connect with other travelers and outdoorists like myself, a space where our voices could be elevated, a space free from the whitewashed narrative typically depicted in the media. Conflicted on how to proceed, I reached out to a few friends and found the encouragement I needed. Finally, one late-summer day, I looked fear in the eyes and empowered myself to speak up in a social media post that launched a movement.

> Vanlife is a PRIVILEGE! There, I said it. To make a choice, you must have a choice. And it's a privilege to choose your lifestyle. Many of us vanlifers are #DigitalNomads with access to remote work. We have the freedom to go anywhere we choose, and we can afford the cost of fuel to get there. The freedom to travel gives us many options. We can purchase healthy food from co-ops, farmers' markets, and niche markets as we travel. We can choose to only eat organic, non-GMO, gluten-free, vegan, pasture-raised. Planet Fitness gym memberships give us access to showers, Wi-Fi, and treadmills. We have the flexibility to explore our hobbies and pursue our passions uninhibited.

> We're not being policed on public lands or arrested in laundromat parking lots (most of us, anyway). But let's be honest, that's because #vanlife is primarily white, and becoming more gentrified every day. And the constant glamorization is driving that more and more.

But let's be real, what are we doing to create a space for underrepresented voices in this growing community? I've been to many gatherings & meetups this year where I was one of few, if not the only, people of color. Am I the only person of color in vanlife?

Hell no! We out here.

So why aren't we hearing more from the marginalized individuals in this community? Why is it only the privileged stories we read about on here? What are the privileged many doing to make this lifestyle safe and accessible for ALL members of our community?

Mmm-hmm. Shit's gotta change, y'all.

Anyway, just me thinking out loud. Y'all will be hearing more from me on this again soon.

#DiversifyVanlife

I typed this while sitting at Angel Peak in the New Mexican Badlands on a warm evening, emotions flooding through the core of my being. As I hit post, a cold shiver went up my spine. With my heart racing and my body shaking, I put my phone down and went for a walk.

The post was not intended to start a movement, nor was I trying to be divisive, as some would go on to suggest. On the contrary, my deep love for this lifestyle and my community drove me to use my voice to bring these harmful issues to the surface. My conscience would no longer allow me to remain silent.

When I returned to my phone, I knew that I was likely to find one of two things: a fierce backlash from the vocal "pillars" of the community or an outpouring of support from those whose experiences aligned with mine. I found both. And, most important, I found the resolve and the courage to speak my truth.

This was the birth of a movement that shifted the narrative: the Diversify Vanlife movement.

DIVERSIFY VANLIFE

Diversify Vanlife started from a place of frustration. After that first incendiary post, many people mobilized around the idea of #DiversifyVanlife. It was a confirmation that I wasn't alone in needing this space. The hashtag led to the creation of the Instagram page @diversify.vanlife.

Since its inception, Diversify Vanlife has been committed to carving out space for underrepresented people in the road travel community while amplifying the voices and stories of those taking up space in the margins—BIPOC, people with disabilities, LGBTQIA+, and those at all intersections. From a post to a hashtag to an Instagram page, a community coalesced around this mission, and it quickly evolved into a movement. For the first time in the vanlife community, BIPOC gained visibility in this lifestyle. Collectively and in solidarity we proclaimed *we don't need permission.*

The Diversify Vanlife community is shifting the narrative of the modern nomadic movement and redefining community for ourselves by prioritizing intersectionality, sustainability, intentional inclusivity, and nature reconnection. For many of us who identify as BIPOC, our connection to nature and the outdoors has been ruptured due to colonization. There's a loss of identity that comes with that, as many of our ancestral and cultural practices are rooted in a connection to the natural world. When we rebuild our connection to nature, we begin to reclaim a sense of belonging and identity.

There are many ways to connect with nature and it will look different for everyone. These are a few tips that have helped me reconnect and begin my healing journey.

- If you have access to information about your ancestral history and traditions, find ways to engage in those practices on the road or in the outdoors as a means of honoring and celebrating your racial or cultural identity—cook cultural dishes, forage, do arts and crafts, practice yoga, go hiking.

- Journal and reflect on your experiences in nature. What comes up for you? How does it make you feel? What outdoor activities make you feel more connected and grounded?

- Share your experiences and reflections with people you trust and feel emotionally safe with.

- Don't be afraid to evolve traditional cultural practices to fit into your life on the road, especially if it grounds you or brings you meaning.

- Connect with the Diversify Vanlife community or other BIPOC vanlifers and outdoorists who can relate to your experiences and share in your journey of healing.

As a community-run organization, we believe that everyone deserves to feel seen and heard, to be represented, and to have access to the outdoors. And we're not alone. Organizations like Vanlife Pride and Outdoorsy Black Women and events like Black Nomads Meet are helping to push for positive change. By using our collective social capital, we hope to continue to advocate for equal representation in a way that empowers other BIPOC and marginalized groups of people to pursue this lifestyle and get outdoors.

The impact Diversify Vanlife has had on the landscape of road travel and the outdoors is substantial, but it hasn't been without challenges. We've been labeled exclusive and divisive by people who don't understand. And this is a common misconception; when marginalized demographics create their own spaces, it often becomes controversial. Black, Indigenous, Asian, and other people of color need their own safe spaces. LGBTQIA+ people need their own safe spaces. We need spaces free from the stereotypes and marginalization that are prevalent in nearly every other space, including vanlife and the outdoors. Having community, support, and recognition gives us permission to show up as our full, authentic selves. We're reclaiming our safe spaces by breaking down barriers that have often infringed upon the freedoms of people who identify as BIPOC. One way we're doing this is by providing practical and accessible resources created by and for the community, like the "Diversify Vanlife BIPOC Guide to Vanlife and the Outdoors." This digital living resource is packed with knowledge covering a multitude of stages for getting started in vanlife, tips for buying and building a rig, essential gear, safety, and much more to empower anyone who lives or wants to live this lifestyle.

Diversify Vanlife centers the voices and experiences of BIPOC at all intersections, but we're not exclusive. Everyone is welcome in our community and allies are needed. Building a safe and welcoming community requires cooperation and a commitment from everyone.

Allyship means:
- Taking on the struggle as your own.
- A commitment to self-education.
- Decentering yourself from the narrative.
- Amplifying the voices of marginalized individuals.
- Using your privilege to push for equality and equity in the spaces you navigate.

Our growing community was founded on an earth love that runs deep. It is fluid and it touches everything we create. From our podcast and blog, to our events and social media, we have finally given greater audiences a more accurate portrayal of what a diverse and inclusive community looks like in the outdoors, and also the proof that BIPOC are taking up space and doing great things.

—Diversify Vanlife

Now that you're here, dear reader, you've been inducted into the Diversify Vanlife community. So, I invite you to take the Diversify Vanlife Road Travel and Outdoor Pledge.

As part of the Diversify Vanlife community, I pledge to:

- Actively work to create inclusive, safe spaces, both outdoor and virtual, for equal-access adventure, exploration, conversation, and community.

- Speak up against racism, sexism, ageism, ableism, homophobia, transphobia, xenophobia, hateful speech, and all other forms of injustice.

- Intentionally listen to and amplify BIPOC and underrepresented voices and leadership.

- Respect the spaces created by and for BIPOC and other marginalized peoples.

- Proactively learn about cultures, identities, communities, land, and Indigenous history while unlearning habits and beliefs that perpetuate conflict, violence, and discrimination against marginalized peoples.

- Commit to minimizing my negative environmental impact.

- Hold community members and myself accountable for continued growth, learning, and positive action.

- Exert my road travel presence with respect for: the land, wildlife, communities, other travelers, and my own body and spirit.

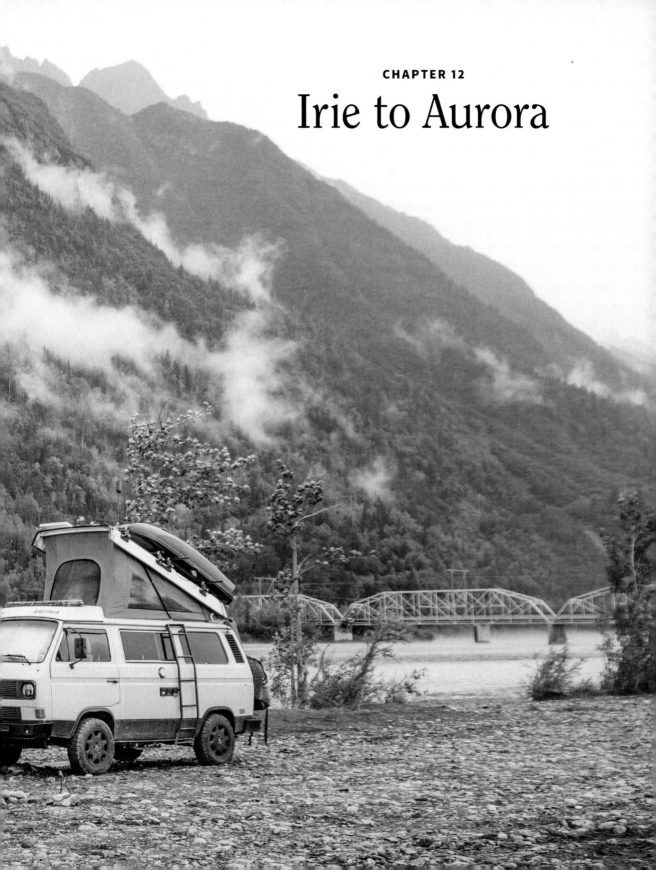

CHAPTER 12

Irie to Aurora

Irie's engine hums with confidence as she carries us north along the twists and turns of the Parks Highway from Anchorage to Talkeetna.

Her wheels hug every curve with extraordinary alacrity as if she were made to sail this smooth asphalt river. I glance over at Dustin, who has a soft, contented smile on his face, one hand resting on the stick shift, the other on the steering wheel, bridging the bond between human and machine. Through the windshield, the field of blue stretches far beyond what my eyes can follow. Up here, in the land of the midnight sun, where the earth bends toward its northern terminus, the fierce golden rays seem to engulf my very soul. Even with sunglasses on, the aura of brightness makes my eyes squint.

Amara, our German Shepherd pup, with her hind legs on the floor and her upper body draped across my lap, hangs her head out the window, a wind-whipped grin on her face. The warm air kisses my skin and I let my mind drift to the low thrum of Irie's wheels on the pavement. Hues of green and white and brown float by as the Alaskan landscape takes shape. These were the visions that permeated my daydreams before life on the road, now manifested in this present moment.

The highway bends again, to the right this time, and without warning Irie nearly careens into a ditch. Awestruck, with eyes wide and mouths agape. There before us, silently present, stands Denali. Unreal. Breathtaking.

There are some mountains that need no explanation, and Denali, the highest peak on the North American continent, is certainly among them.

THE DAWN

I've dreamt of seeing Alaska ever since I was a child in Trinidad. I used to watch National Geographic documentaries on my parents' small black-and-white television (yeah, the box with the bunny ears on top—remember those?), in awe that such a place existed. My mind would race with visions of Noami the explorer skating across glaciers and touching snow-capped peaks, the aurora borealis dancing overhead. The idea

of breathing the cold mountain air and trekking the vast evergreen forests, distinctly foreign from the coconut palm–lined roads and consistently warm tropical climate of my tiny island, imbued my youthful imagination with fantastical wonder.

The profound calling stuck with me, influencing the trajectory of my life, and inspiring my love for science, nature, and travel. Decades later, as Dustin and I sat cross-legged on the floor in our disheveled New Orleans apartment planning our once-in-a-lifetime road trip, a map of North America spread before us, my eyes pulled to the top left corner: *Alaska.*

Even though the possibility of reaching Alaska was at my fingertips for the first time, it felt like a far-fetched dream. I was still living according to some societal plan. If I worked hard enough and achieved a certain level of success, I thought, perhaps someday I could reward myself with Alaska, but not before. As I sat on the cold tile floor, on the precipice of driving off society's road map, I asked myself, *Why not?* With this shift, I began my new journey, the sole artist and creator of my life's trajectory.

So the agreement was made: a one-year road trip from New Orleans to Alaska to experience the aurora borealis then back to our regularly scheduled lives. Thus, Irie to Aurora was born. And as you know, our one-year road trip shed its limitations.

THE ROAD TO ALASKA

In 2019, plans were beginning to coalesce for us to finally make it to Alaska. Dustin and I had established a thriving remote business and were confident in our ability to fully sustain ourselves on the road. We spent that winter in New Orleans overhauling Irie to prepare her for the trek across Canada and up the Alcan Highway. We planned to hit the road north in the spring of 2020, but a few days before we were set to leave, the COVID-19 pandemic hit in full force and the world effectively shut down. With the uncertainty of the days/weeks/months ahead, we were left debating what would be the responsible thing to do as travelers. Ultimately, we decided to put our plans for Alaska on hold. It left us wondering if we would ever make it there.

During that first year of the pandemic, Dustin and I bounced between friends with land who were gracious enough to let us park Irie, and public lands (the areas that were still open) where we could isolate. It was a scary and lonely time. Sharing campfires with friends or strangers was a big risk that we weren't willing to take. And the inability to make those connections brought back similar feelings of loneliness that recalled our first few months on the road. The only difference: We were sure, now more than ever, that our decision to live in a van was the right one for us.

In the early months of 2021, there were talks of reopening the border between the US and Canada. This reignited our plans of making the trek to Alaska. Travel restrictions were still unpredictable so we knew we would have to be flexible. But at this point in our vanlife journey, we were already schooled in releasing expectations for outcomes and going with the flow.

With anticipation of crossing the border from Montana and traversing Alberta and British Columbia, we slowly made our way north to big sky country. As each month went by from January to June, we were hopeful that the border would reopen. And each month we were disappointed by another delay. The continuous setbacks made us anxious that we would miss our window to get to Alaska since the ideal time for van travel up north is brief, from June to August. Still, we stuck to our plans. But after another crushing border delay in June, we decided to rethink our mode of travel and take a ferry on the Alaska Marine Highway, bypassing the bulk of Canada.

The ferry to Alaska departs from Bellingham, Washington. And with a couple of weeks to get there, we thought we'd have time for a quick detour through Glacier National Park in Montana, which is a place we'd always wanted to visit. But a close encounter with a brown bear who forgot to look both ways before crossing the road threatened to derail our plans once again.

On our first day in the park, we planned a scenic drive on Going-to-the-Sun Road—a narrow two-lane mountain highway snaking from one side of the park to the other. The fifty-mile crossing is one of a kind, lined with jagged mountains, cascading waterfalls, deep valleys, stunning glaciers, and an abundance of wildlife. As we descended the eastern slope of the mountain pass, Dustin behind the wheel and Amara in her usual spot on my lap, head out the window, a brown bear darted out from the trees into the road a few feet in front of us. I yelped, "BEAR!" and without a moment's hesitation, Dustin stomped Irie's brake pedal to the floor and spun the wheel just enough to narrowly miss the bear, who quickly disappeared into the woods on the other side. We rolled to a stop in a nearby pullout with smoke and fluids billowing from the undercarriage, the three of us shaking with adrenaline. Fortunately, the only casualty of this incident was the hydrau-

lic brake system, which left Irie stranded at the local VW spa and service center. (An annoying and expensive setback, for sure.) But a week later, an eccentric mechanic blessed our beloved Irie with a clean bill of health and we put our wheels in motion again (cue Willie Nelson's "On the Road Again").

The first leg of our road trip took us seven hundred miles along scenic highways and byways, from Glacier, Montana, to Bellingham, Washington, where we traded vanlife for boat life on an unforgettable voyage through Alaska's mysterious Inside Passage. Irie's wheels left the

Vanagon enthusiast excitedly recommended the ferry up the Inside Passage, calling it a once-in-a-lifetime experience. He said the ferry is often referred to as the poor man's Alaska cruise because you can walk on with nothing but a backpack and pitch a tent on the third-floor deck. For us, however, this might as well have been a luxury liner. We slept in a two-berth cabin, bathed twice a day in our private shower, and dined on genuine Alaskan fare—fresh halibut, smoked salmon, reindeer sausage. And a Trini chef named Steve gave this Trini gyal a little taste of home all the way up north.

As we sailed from the tumultuous open ocean to the emerald waters of the Hecate Strait, it looked like we floated right into a giant Bob Ross painting. We zigzagged the treacherous Wrangell Narrows by day and passed into the fjord-lined Lynn Canal under cover of a blue-black night. A half dozen landings along the way gave us a chance to stretch our sea legs and explore sleepy fishing communities. Three bald eagles soaring together overhead bid us "Welcome to Alaska" on our first stop in Ketchikan. The fresh, salty sea air made me nostalgic for my childhood village life. But the glacier-laden mountains that flanked every twist and turn reminded me constantly that *this ain't no Carnival cruise*. Porpoises, whales, otters, eagles, and seals were joyful daily sightings. And the warm reflections of tangerine sunsets on the quivering sea signaled to me that everythin' irie.

pavement as we rolled into the belly of the MV *Matanuska*, a four-hundred-foot-long ferry with 7,200 horsepower, a massive floating vessel. From the bow of the ship, we waved goodbye to the Lower 48 with Mount Rainier standing proudly in the distance, bidding us a fond farewell. It was thrilling to finally be so close to this dream, but I was mostly relieved because everything that could stand in our way did, yet there we were, on a boat to Alaska, with Irie resting safely below deck, for once just along for the ride.

We first learned of the Alaska Marine Highway a few years prior, when a friend and fellow

Most of my time aboard was spent walking the rails, binoculars and telephoto lens in hand, revel-

ing in the beauty of the moment with my diverse ad hoc community of backpackers, retirees, locals, a college grad returning home to Juneau, messy-haired and scruffy-faced ramblers like us, and our twenty-four-hour crew on this working vessel.

Our Irie had come a long way since she began her maiden voyage from New Orleans to Alaska. From a stock thirty-year-old van to a full-blown adventure rig. For us all to finally be there, to see it in person, was surreal. And to drive Irie off the MV *Matanuska* and onto the Alaskan shore filled me with pride.

Our summer in Alaska was brief and adventurous, two months altogether, until the leaves changed color and the air turned brisk. In that time, I had many firsts—I hiked on a massive glacier, fly-fished for salmon in emerald-green water in Haines, foraged for wild berries in Hatcher Pass, and explored Denali by floatplane. I celebrated my birthday in late August with a backpacking trip to see Bear Glacier, but the sixty-mile-per-hour wind gusts made the final leg of the trek too treacherous to summit. On workdays, our mobile office views were never stale; we'd nestle Irie on the banks of rushing glacier-fed rivers, with views of mountain ranges that seemed to go on forever. When the September rains came, signaling the end of summer, we made preparations for our return south via the Alcan Highway. But not before one more adventure.

I'll never forget the first time I laid eyes on this little tan van, sitting proudly in the driveway, nose pointing to the road, ready for her next adventure. Five years and a million miles later, I finally stood atop Irie, the tan Vanagon with the bright blue canopy, flanked by the iridescent green radiance of the northern lights. With fingers numbed by the early-autumn chill, I wiped away tears of elation from my cheeks. *Dreams do come true . . .*

I was stunned by the thought as it flashed through my mind. Even though I was always a dreamer, this idea was a luxury I was never allowed to entertain. The realities of my upbringing required a strict focus on practical, realistic goals

to survive. And the hard, sometimes harsh limitations of that life made the dreamer mindset a dangerous and unattainable fantasy. But as I stood there bathing in the magic of the moment, my heart yielded to the truth of those words. Maybe it was the pragmatism of my childhood and the idealism of being a dreamer that anchored me on my path. Or maybe I'm just one of the lucky ones. Either way, this dream came true in ways I could not have anticipated.

Dustin joined me on Irie's rooftop patio and wrapped his arms around me. Gazing at the lightshow happening above, he asked, "What's next?" I squished in closer to him and whispered, "I don't know, but we don't have to figure it out right now."

OVERVIEW OF OUR ROUTE TO ALASKA

Our road trip from Glacier, Montana, to Talkeetna, Alaska, took us on an estimated 2,800 miles of scenic highways, byways, and waterways, providing ample opportunities for outdoor activities—hiking, swimming, hot springs, rafting, biking, camping, fishing, wildlife viewing, and so much more. And we immersed ourselves in local food and culture with stops in the many quaint and quirky towns along the way. This wasn't the route we had planned initially, but with the closure of the US-Canada border, it was the most practical. It also turned out to be the most scenic and adventurous road trip we've ever taken.

Glacier, Montana, to Talkeetna, Alaska
(~2,800 miles)

First Leg: Scenic Highways & Byways

GLACIER, MONTANA, TO BELLINGHAM, WASHINGTON (~700 MILES BY ROAD)

MONTANA HIGHWAY 93

West Glacier, Montana, to Eureka, Montana

Key Stops:

Glacier National Park
- Sunrise on Lake McDonald
- Drive Going-to-the-Sun Road
- Boating and swimming at Saint Mary Lake

LAKE KOOCANUSA SCENIC BYWAY

Eureka, Montana, to Libby, Montana

Key Stops:
- Photography at Koocanusa Lake and Bridge
- Swimming at Peck Gulch

A PORTION OF THE INTERNATIONAL SELKIRK LOOP

Bonners Ferry, Idaho, to Sandpoint, Idaho
  (aka Wild Horse Trail Scenic Byway)
Sandpoint, Idaho, to Newport, Washington
Newport, Washington, to Tiger, Washington

Key Stops:
- Bird-watching in Kootenai National Wildlife Refuge
- Swimming in the Pend Oreille River outside of Newport

SELKIRK MOUNTAINS TO KETTLE FALLS

Tiger, Washington, to Kettle Falls, Washington

Key Stops:
- Frater Lake Rest Area
- Crystal Falls
- Little Pend Oreille National Wildlife Refuge

SHERMAN PASS SCENIC BYWAY

Kettle Falls, Washington, to Republic,
 Washington

Key Stops:

◦ Fresh cider and huckleberry shakes at the Old
 Apple Warehouse

NORTH CASCADES SCENIC HIGHWAY

Winthrop, Washington, to Sedro-Woolley,
 Washington

Key Stops:

◦ Hike Washington Pass Overlook Trail
◦ Take in the view at Ross Lake and Diablo Lake
 Overlooks

**CHUCKANUT DRIVE
(AKA THE ORIGINAL PACIFIC COAST HIGHWAY,
AKA WASHINGTON'S BIG SUR)**

Burlington, Washington, to Bellingham,
 Washington

Key Stops:

◦ Eat fresh raw oysters at the Chuckanut Oyster
 Bar
◦ Hike Oyster Dome Trail

Second Leg: The Inside Passage
BELLINGHAM, WASHINGTON, TO SKAGWAY, ALASKA

THE INSIDE PASSAGE VIA THE ALASKA MARINE HIGHWAY (~1,200 MILES BY SEA)

Tip: Bring a good set of binoculars and a telephoto lens

Key Stops:
- A stroll through Ketchikan to stretch your sea legs
- Tour the town of Sitka
- Fly-fishing in Haines
- Walking tour of historic Skagway

Third Leg: Mainland Alaska
SKAGWAY, ALASKA, TO TALKEETNA, ALASKA (~900 MILES BY ROAD)

KLONDIKE HIGHWAY

Skagway, Alaska, to British Columbia border, Canada

British Columbia to the Yukon border, Canada

Yukon border to Whitehorse, Yukon, Canada (joins the Alcan Highway)

ALCAN HIGHWAY

Whitehorse, Yukon, Canada, to Tok, Alaska

ALASKA HIGHWAY 1 (TOK HIGHWAY/GLENN HIGHWAY)

Tok, Alaska, to Palmer, Alaska

ALASKA HIGHWAY 3 (PARKS HIGHWAY)

Palmer, Alaska, to Talkeetna, Alaska (Gateway to Denali National Park)

Final Thoughts

Well, dear reader, here we are. We've reached the end of the book but not the end of the journey. As we say in Trinidad, "The journey now start."

It took me five years to get from New Orleans to Alaska in Irie. And between the blood, sweat, and tears from all the breakdowns and the obstacles and meltdowns from reinventing myself in an unconventional lifestyle, I questioned my life decision at least a hundred times. In these low moments, when fear and self-doubt undermined my resolve, I couldn't help but think, *Was any of this worth it?* and *How badly have I screwed up my life?* Because it hasn't all been great. In fact, as I was putting the finishing touches on the photography curation for this book, my hard drive crashed the day after the backup hard drive failed (what are the odds?), taking with it a month's worth of my work. And to boot, Irie's rear axle fell off twice that same weekend, leaving us stranded while on a photo shoot to fill the blank pages.

As I sat at the side of a lonely highway, tears of hopelessness streaming down my face, I remembered the summer of 2019 when Irie's engine gave up the ghost. We were driving up a mountain pass somewhere in Colorado when the sound of the straining motor dropped several octaves. Irie began to slow down until our momentum finally ran out, sending us rolling backward for nearly a mile to the nearest pullout. After consulting several Westy mechanics, we were forced to accept the prognosis: Irie would need a new engine.

At the time, I was working on passion projects and transitioning into a new career, so we were still dependent on Dustin's income from his part-time remote job. The cost of a new engine was far more than we had saved and, with few financial prospects on the horizon, our options were slim. We scrutinized every possibility, including selling Irie and going back to New Orleans to start over. Finally, during one long, melancholy night sitting beside a campfire, we made the impetuous decision to order the engine and put it all on a credit card. That was it. From that moment we were fully committed to a thirty-year-old van with a history of expensive breakdowns. But then, shortly after getting Irie humming again, I managed to secure a lucrative photography contract and Dustin landed a long-term freelance gig. And once again, *everythin' was irie*.

I think a lot about how society defines failure as the result of not achieving a goal or meeting an expectation. When I was adjusting to life on the road, one of my greatest struggles was overcoming feelings of failure from leaving behind my career to pursue an alternative lifestyle. And in the summer of 2019, when we were contemplating selling the van and going back to New Orleans, my biggest fear was that friends and loved ones would see me as a failure because I didn't stick with vanlife. I was operating under the idea that permanently pursuing whatever path you started on is the only way to avoid failure and achieve success. But this view makes failure, and success for that matter, contingent upon the outcome.

The American Dream, which I've touched upon numerous times throughout this book, is based on this "destination view" of success. But for many millennials, myself included, our success revolves around the freedom to change, to choose our own path, and try new things. For me, the American Dream is being able to say *I'm not done with this dream so I'm gonna keep going despite the obstacles* or *This dream isn't working for me anymore so I'm gonna do something different*. It's having the freedom to reinvent myself over and over again as many times as I want, which is what I've done throughout my life on the road.

Redefining the American Dream is redefining what it means to be successful. It's recognizing the journey as equal to or perhaps more important than the destination itself.

Society tells us that we need to have a road map for our lives, a view of the outcome before we even get started. Following our deepest desires can be terrifying when they lead us off of that path, especially when the new path is filled with uncertainty. Fear of the unknown can often make us feel powerless and vulnerable, sending us into a downward spiral of anxiety and self-doubt. And constantly contemplating what-ifs and imagined defeats can be debilitating, causing us to never take action. But as I look back on my decision to pursue vanlife, I can't help but wonder how my life would have been if I never had the tenacity to go after my dreams, to take that giant leap into the unknown. For me, that's the most terrifying and powerless feeling I can imagine.

Today my vanlife journey continues, with Dustin and Amara, of course. Irie's wheels are still rolling, still going wherever the road takes us. We still have breakdowns and meltdowns, but now I no longer question if it's the end of my journey. Because I've learned that no matter what happens, it's just another milepost along the road that I'm paving for myself. And who knows, maybe someday I'll trade in my beloved van for a plot of land with a tiny house and raise chickens and goats and grow a vegetable garden. Until then, I welcome all the lessons and growth still to come.

Acknowledgments

I always dreamt of writing a book, but I never imagined it would happen so soon. This journey has proven to be much harder than I anticipated, but in the end, it's been one of the most rewarding experiences of my life. And there are so many people to thank:

To my mom, Ursilla: There are no words to express how grateful I am to be your daughter. So many of my childhood memories are filled with love and all the sweet things you did for me. I know it wasn't easy to watch me board that airplane all those years ago, but you supported me anyway. Thank you for believing in me and encouraging me to trust my intuition and to go after my dreams with conviction. I couldn't have done it without your love and support, and the many lessons you taught me. I'll never forget that melancholy morning in my New Orleans apartment when I was contemplating this wild dream of vanlife; through all the self-doubt, your words empowered me to get up

and go after it. For that, I am ever grateful. I love you, Ma; you are appreciated.

Grandma Mary, I miss you. I know you're resting well. Thank you for your gift of storytelling and imagination. I'm grounded by your wisdom and love, and I can never thank you enough for the cultural and spiritual values you instilled in me.

Miriam, my beautiful sister, your support means the world to me.

To my partner, Dustin, thank you for always being down with my wild ideas and for accepting me for me. You have my heartfelt appreciation and gratitude for sharing in this adventure with me, and my thanks for your love and support along the way. This book wouldn't be what it is without all your dedication and time—late nights brainstorming, being my cameraman and my first editor. Thank you for your words of encouragement in my moments of self-doubt, and for reminding me that I am deserving of all the blessings I receive. Life on the road wouldn't be the same without you and Amara. You are a blessing in my life. I love you, babe.

Big shout-out and sincere thanks to my Diversify Vanlife family—Faren, Rachel, Ola, Mohit, Wynne, and Bess—for all your continued work and dedication to DV and for collaborating and creating the sacred space we're carving out together as a community. I continue to learn so much from all of you. Faren and Rachel, I'm especially grateful for your time reviewing and line-editing my manuscript, and for your honest feedback. Love and gratitude always. To my dear friend Jayme Serbell, thank you for reminding me that I can't pour from an empty cup. Deenaalee Hodgdon, thank you for your wise counsel and steadfast leadership, and for lending your powerful voice to this book.

To my in-laws, thank you for your continued love and support, especially in those early years of vanlife. You helped make the transition far less daunting.

I'd be remiss if I didn't mention the hardworking team at GoWesty, who have helped keep our Irie rolling all these years. Thank you for your passion, love, and dedication to keeping these iconic vessels on the road. It's truly a love affair.

I would like to express a special thanks to the Simon Element team for all your hard work bringing this book to life. To my editor, Ronnie Alvarado, thank you for taking a chance on me and for sharing your vision. I'm truly grateful for the experience and for your patience, guidance, and continual support.

To the Diversify Vanlife community, thank you all for inspiring me to dream out loud. Ase'. To the Kift community and team—Colin, Lauren, Cam, John, Mo, Jade, and Nick—thank you for showing up and for your support and patience as I completed my manuscript. Special thanks to Sante for bringing us together—you are a visionary, my friend.

To the anonymous community members who shared so vulnerably and openly from their lived experiences, thank you. I sincerely believe your stories are the ones that need to be told.

Thank you to all the folks who stopped to offer help on the many occasions that Dustin and I were broken down at the side of the road. You've each played a role in our journey and reminded us time and again why we chose this lifestyle. How wild and wonderful this journey has been.

Thank you to all the Ancestors. I stand on your shoulders.

APPENDIX A
Vanlife Road Trip

TIPS FOR PLANNING & PREPARING FOR A VANLIFE ROAD TRIP

My love for road-tripping was a big influence on my decision to move into a van. I've taken many such journeys, and if there's one thing I've learned, it's that having a good plan can be the difference between being safe and stress-free or stranded on a lonely highway with no cell signal. Planning your trip can save you time and money, minimize unforeseen circumstances, and help you prioritize the kind of experience you want to have. Below is a compilation of tips, checklists, and things to consider that have helped me to plan all my road trips. And you don't have to live in a van to take advantage of this list. Just choose a destination and always extensively research the location you're traveling to. Happy travels!

Factors to consider and things to do:

- Activities and experiences at the destination.

- Climate and road conditions.

- Decide how long the road trip will be.

- Set your pace. Consider your travel style and be realistic about your time. Will you practice slow travel? Are you working as you go?

- Add in must-see stops you'd like to make and for how long.

- Book campsites or lodging and activities like guided tours in advance, especially in popular areas.

- Set a budget.

- Estimate the cost of fuel based on the number of miles to your destination (and back, if you'll be returning). Add an extra percentage for detours and scenic routes.

- Consider lodging (paid campgrounds, dispersed, or Airbnb), food (eating out or

- Consider where you'll sleep each night. We enjoy dispersed camping, so we plan our route to take advantage of public lands.

- Identify alternative routes in case road conditions require a detour.

- Build in extra time.

- Allow time for unforeseen incidents like breakdowns as well as rest stops and spontaneous detours. Think of any other factors that may affect your travel time; for example, Irie's cruising speed is slower than the average car on the road, so we adjust our time estimate to account for it.

- Take time to unwind along the journey, to slow down and enjoy the little things. What's a road trip without taking the time to enjoy the beauty along the way?

cooking in your rig), and the cost of activities and attractions.

- Keep a contingency fund in case of breakdowns or unforeseen expenses.

- Plan your route, as a good plan helps maximize adventure and minimize excess driving time.

- Research the stops you want to make and plug them into a mapping app. We use Google Maps, plugging in multiple stops to get an approximate route, then we highlight the route on our road atlas or a paper map.

- Prepare for border crossings: If you'll be crossing international borders, be sure you understand all requirements and comply with regulations. Don't forget your passport, and keep your passport and driver's license up to date at all times.

- Check travel advisories and restrictions.

- Be mindful of insurance policies. Most vehicle and health insurance policies only cover travel in the home country. Supplementary vehicle insurance may be required. It's also a good idea to purchase travel insurance when traveling internationally.

- Make a packing list and add the essentials first.

- Bring clothing for any type of weather conditions and activities.

- Add camping gear and digital gear you'll need for the trip.

- If you're traveling with kids or pets, create a packing list for them, too.

- Basic Road Trip Packing List:
  - camping chairs and table
  - awning/outdoor shelter
  - solar shower
  - water filter or purifier
  - hammock
  - stove and cooking utensils
  - bed and blankets

TRAVELING WITH A DOG

When Amara, our German Shepherd pup, joined our pack, our lives changed in so many beautiful ways. She's a constant reminder of why we chose this lifestyle, as she keeps us seeking new and exciting adventures, provides a constant source of entertainment, and shows us every day what unconditional love looks like. Adding a dog to our vanlife was the best decision Dustin and I made since getting on the road back in 2016. But traveling with a furry friend also comes with a lot of responsibilities and requires some extra preparation. Use the list below to help to ensure your travel companion stays safe, comfortable, and happy on the road.

- Consider the climate you'll be traveling through and to, and ensure your rig is equipped to keep your furry friend comfortable, especially in hot climates.

- Create a packing list for your companion and include climate-appropriate gear, toys, medication, and treats.

- Get a vet checkup before travel and ensure your animal is microchipped. Pack their vaccination records and any other important documents.

- If traveling internationally with a dog, you may need additional documentation. Check the requirements for the country you're traveling to and/or through.

- Consider slow travel and make plenty of stops for them to stretch their legs, exercise, and sniff the ground. Stopping at dog parks on your travel route is a great way for your pup to burn off some excess energy.

- Save space in the budget for a doggy sitter whenever the adventure is not dog friendly.

- When booking lodging, make sure it's dog friendly. Some campgrounds and RV parks don't allow dogs.

- Plan dog-friendly adventures. Trails in national parks do not allow dogs and many other trails require dogs to be leashed.

- Dog Road Trip Packing List
  - travel dog bowls
  - leash and harness
  - extra poop bags
  - cooling gear (for warm climates)
  - warm gear (for cool climates)
  - rain gear
  - comfy dog bed
  - collar light for nighttime
  - favorite toys
  - favorite treats
  - extra food and water
  - medication and flea and tick prevention
  - brush or comb, and for dogs with hair, not fur, haircut tools

PREPARING YOUR RIG

Nothing can derail a road trip quicker than vehicle trouble and Dustin and I have been through it all with our Irie on the road. The experiences I share in this book barely scratch the surface of our breakdown sagas. You could say that our early years on the road were a dry run for our trip to Alaska. Each breakdown was an opportunity to make an upgrade to our thirtysomething-year-old rig, so by the time we planned our preeminent road trip to Alaska, we were confident that she was mechanically sound. Still, we could never account for every unforeseen situation that may arise. But with some preparation, the right tools, and a lot of spare parts, we can be ready for almost anything. And it helps that Dustin has become somewhat of an amateur mechanic these years on the road with Irie.

Use the thorough list below as a checklist to prepare your rig for a road trip.

- Get a full mechanical checkup.

- Always have your rig inspected and serviced by a competent, trusted mechanic prior to taking any long-distance road trip.

- Have a basic understanding of how your vehicle operates and how to use the tools listed below. Learn how to:
    - Check and refill your oil, coolant, and other fluids.
    - Use a jack and change a tire.
    - Jump-start a dead battery.
    - Replace a belt.
    - Replace or repair a coolant hose.

- A basic tool kit is essential for any vanlife road trip and should include the following (at a minimum):
    - jumper cables
    - tow strap
    - socket wrench and sockets
    - crescent wrench/spanner
    - rubber mallet or hammer
    - screwdrivers (Phillips head and flat head)
    - a set of combination wrenches
    - wheel chocks
    - hazard indicators
    - mechanic's gloves
    - self-fusing silicone tape (for sealing radiator hose leaks)

    - hose clamps, zip ties, and steel wire
    - nuts, bolts, and washers
    - duct tape and electrical tape
    - hand cleaner and shop towel
    - a bottle of fuel system cleaner (Irie got a tank of bad gas in Canada. A bottle of Sea Foam Motor Treatment saved us.)
    - a spare tire and jack. Make sure your spare tire is in good condition and all components for the jack are accounted for (jack handle, lug wrench, etc.).

- The spare parts you carry will depend on the age, model, and condition of your rig. Irie is a classic vehicle and parts are hard to come by, so we keep a variety of spare parts in the van.

But even mechanically sound, newer-model rigs break down from time to time, and most breakdowns are caused by something simple and easy to replace. These spare parts could save you from being stranded.

- spare belts (number and type vary by vehicle)
- radiator hoses (cooling hoses)
- a spare lug nut or bolt
- spark plugs
- distributor cap and rotor
- fuel filter
- fuel pump
- fuses
- bulbs
- motor oil, brake fluid, and transmission fluid
- While it may not be essential for all road trips, carrying a twelve-volt air compressor is a good idea. In lieu of an air compressor, carry a can of Fix-A-Flat, as it may come in handy in a pinch.
- fuel can with extra fuel
- jump-starter battery pack

- Make sure all vehicle documents are up to date (insurance, registration, etc.). Print out the insurance card so you don't have to hand your phone to a police officer when they ask for proof of insurance.

- Store copies of important documents in a safe place away from your vehicle, and never (NEVER) keep the title in the vehicle.

- Sign up for roadside assistance coverage through your insurance company or AAA (our AAA Premier membership has saved us more times than I can count).

- Have a trusted mechanic you can call for advice.

- food storage

- cooler or fridge

- water storage

- drinking and cooking water

- water for washing dishes and showering

Glossary

Adventure mobile: a home-on-wheels; a vehicle for travel and exploration.

Conversion: to modify or retrofit a van or other vehicle into a habitable home.

Developed camping: the act of camping in established and maintained campgrounds with designated sites.

Digital nomad: an individual who earns a living while traveling.

Dispersed camping: the act of camping on public lands outside of designated campgrounds.

Entrepreneur: a self-employed business owner.

Freelancer: a self-employed worker who typically works on a project-by-project basis and is responsible for their own taxes and insurance.

Full-timer: a classification of vanlifer whose vehicle serves as their primary, year-round residence.

Hippie: (popularized in the 1960s) a person leading an unconventional life, often associated with counterculture and a rejection of conventional societal norms.

Home-on-wheels: converted vehicle, built out with certain comforts that make it home.

Houseless: having no physical, stationary dwelling; may be by choice or out of necessity.

Modern nomad: an individual opting to forgo a stationary home in favor of a life of travel.

Outdoorist: an individual who enjoys spending time in nature; a nature lover; may be an advocate for environmental causes.

Overland digital nomad: someone who uses technology to earn an income while traveling and working remotely from the road.

Overlanding: to travel by land in a van or vehicle.

Part-timer: a classification of vanlifer who maintains roots in a stationary location, typically having a permanent or stationary home, and spends several weeks, months, or full seasons living and traveling in their rig.

Public lands: land owned by local, state, or federal government that is available for recreation and use by private individuals, often free of charge. Often utilized by vanlifers for camping and recreation.

Remote employee: a full- or part-time employee of an organization who works from home or from any remote location away from the company's office. Also referred to as a traditional employee or W-2 employee.

Rig: a van or vehicle.

Road traveler: anyone who travels over land.

Skoolie: a school bus converted into a home.

Slow travel: an approach to travel that emphasizes connection to local cultures and communities; often synonymous with sustainable travel.

Stealth camping: the act of secretly camping in unestablished locations, with the goal of going undetected.

Vagabond: a person who wanders.

Vandweller: someone who lives in a van or vehicle; vanlifer.

Vandwelling: to live in a van or vehicle.

Vanlife: the act of living in a van; vandwelling.

Vanlifer: someone who dwells or lives in a vehicle.

Wanderlust: a deep desire to explore or travel.

Weekender: weekend warrior; a classification of vanlifer who lives in their primary, stationary residence for reasons such as work, school, or family commitments, taking advantage of weekends, holidays, and vacations to travel and adventure.

APPENDIX C
Native Land Acknowledgments

The Indigenous nations referenced in relation to the photos in this book were adapted from the website Native-land.ca. To learn more about the Indigenous Peoples of North America, their histories, and their cultures, visit Native-land.ca or individual tribal websites.

Cover photo: Ancestral lands of the Newe (Western Shoshone), Eastern Mono/Monache, and Numu (Northern Paiute) Peoples.

Introduction, photo 1: Ancestral lands of the Pueblos and Nuwuvi (Southern Paiute) Peoples.

Chapter 1, photo 1: Ancestral lands of the Newe (Western Shoshone), Cahuilla, and Yuhaviatam/Maarenga'yam (Serrano) Peoples.

Chapter 1, photo 2: Ancestral lands of the Awaswas, Ohlone, and Popeloutchom (Amah Mutsun) Peoples.

Chapter 1, photo 3: Ancestral lands of the Chahta Yakni (Choctaw) Peoples.

Chapter 1, photo 4: Ancestral lands of the Cheyenne, Eastern Shoshone, and Shoshone-Bannock Peoples.

Chapter 1, photo 5: Ancestral lands of the Newe (Western Shoshone), Eastern Mono/Monache, and Numu (Northern Paiute) Peoples.

Chapter 1, photo 6: Ancestral lands of the Cahuilla and Xawiłł Kwñchawaay (Cocopah) Peoples.

Chapter 2, photo 1: Ancestral lands of the Hohokam, Sobaipuri, Akimel O'odham (Upper Pima), Tohono O'odham, and O'odham Jeweḍ Peoples.

Chapter 2, photo 2: Ancestral lands of the Pericú Peoples.

Chapter 2, photo 3: Ancestral lands of the Pueblos and Nuwuvi (Southern Paiute) Peoples.

Chapter 2, photo 4: Ancestral lands of the Núu-agha-tu̱vu̱-pu̱ (Ute), Pueblos, Diné Bikéyah, and Hopitutskwa Peoples.

Chapter 3, photo 1: Ancestral lands of the Hohokam, Pueblos, Hopitutskwa, Yavapaiv Apache, and Ndee/Nnēē (Western Apache) Peoples.

Chapter 3, photo 2: Ancestral lands of the Núu-agha-tu̱vu̱-pu̱ (Ute), Pueblos, and Nuwuvi (Southern Paiute) Peoples.

Chapter 3, photo 3: Ancestral lands of the Pericú Peoples.

Chapter 3, photo 4: Ancestral lands of the Ktunaxa Peoples.

Chapter 3, photo 5: Ancestral lands of the Tübatulabal and Yokuts Peoples.

Chapter 4, photo 1: Ancestral lands of the Núu-agha-tʉvʉ-pʉ (Ute), Pueblos, Diné Bikéyah, and Hopitutskwa Peoples.

Chapter 4, photo 2: Ancestral lands of the Tübatulabal and Yokuts Peoples.

Chapter 4, photos 3–7: Ancestral lands of the Pueblos and Nuwuvi (Southern Paiute) Peoples.

Chapter 5, photo 1: Ancestral lands of the Newe (Western Shoshone), Eastern Mono/Monache, and Numu (Northern Paiute) Peoples.

Chapter 5, photo 2: Ancestral lands of the Pueblos and Nuwuvi (Southern Paiute) Peoples.

Chapter 5, photo 3: Ancestral lands of the Hualapai, Nuwuvi (Southern Paiute), and Pipa Aha Macav (Mojave) Peoples.

Chapter 5, photo 4: Ancestral lands of the Núu-agha-tʉvʉ-pʉ (Ute), Pueblos, and Nuwuvi (Southern Paiute) Peoples.

Chapter 5, photo 5: Ancestral lands of the Wašišiw (Washoe) Peoples.

Chapter 6, photo 1: Ancestral lands of the Newe (Western Shoshone), Eastern Mono/Monache, and Numu (Northern Paiute) Peoples.

Chapter 6, photo 2: Ancestral lands of the Newe (Western Shoshone) Peoples.

Chapter 6, photo 3: Ancestral lands of the Nuwuvi (Southern Paiute), Pueblos, and Núu-agha-tʉvʉ-pʉ (Ute) Peoples.

Chapter 6, photo 4: Ancestral lands of the Newe (Western Shoshone) and Yuhaviatam/Maarenga'yam (Serrano) Peoples.

Chapter 6, photo 5: Ancestral lands of the Núu-agha-tʉvʉ-pʉ (Ute) Peoples.

Chapter 6, photo 6: Ancestral lands of the Eastern Mono/Monache, Western Mono/Monache, and Numu (Northern Paiute) Peoples.

Chapter 6, photo 7: Ancestral lands of the Pueblos and Nuwuvi (Southern Paiute) Peoples.

Chapter 7, photo 1: Ancestral lands of the Núu-agha-tʉvʉ-pʉ (Ute), Pueblos, Diné Bikéyah, and Hopitutskwa Peoples.

Chapter 7, photo 2: Ancestral lands of the Newe (Western Shoshone) and Yuhaviatam/Maarenga'yam (Serrano) Peoples.

Chapter 7, photo 3: Ancestral lands of the Dena'ina Ełnena and Dënéndeh Peoples.

Chapter 7, photo 4: Ancestral lands of the Newe (Western Shoshone), Eastern Mono/Monache, and Numu (Northern Paiute) Peoples.

Chapter 8, photo 1: Ancestral lands of the Newe (Western Shoshone), Eastern Mono/Monache, and Numu (Northern Paiute) Peoples.

Chapter 8, photo 2: Ancestral lands of the Nuwuvi (Southern Paiute), Pueblos, and Núu-agha-tʉvʉ-pʉ (Ute) Peoples.

Chapter 8, photo 3: Ancestral lands of the Pueblos and Nuwuvi (Southern Paiute) Peoples.

Chapter 8, photo 4: Ancestral lands of the Cahuilla and Xawiłł Kwñchawaay (Cocopah) Peoples.

Chapter 8, photo 5: Ancestral lands of the Shoshone-Bannock Peoples.

Chapter 8, photo 6: Ancestral lands of the Cahuilla and Xawiłł Kwñchawaay (Cocopah) Peoples.

Chapter 9, photo 1: Ancestral lands of the Hualapai Peoples.

Chapter 9, photo 2: Ancestral lands of the Newe (Western Shoshone) Peoples.

Chapter 9, photo 3: Ancestral lands of the Newe (Western Shoshone) Peoples.

Chapter 9, photo 4: Ancestral lands of the Newe (Western Shoshone) Peoples.

Chapter 9, photo 5: Ancestral lands of the Hohokam, Sobaipuri, Akimel O'odham (Upper Pima), Tohono O'odham, and O'odham Jeweḍ Peoples.

Chapter 9, photo 6: Ancestral lands of the Pueblos and Nuwuvi (Southern Paiute) Peoples.

Chapter 10, photo 1: Ancestral lands of the Pueblos and Nuwuvi (Southern Paiute) Peoples.

Chapter 10, photo 2: Ancestral lands of the Kojomk'awi (Konkow) Peoples.

Chapter 10, photo 3: Ancestral lands of the Coast Yuki Peoples.

Chapter 10, photo 4: Ancestral lands of the Nuwuvi (Southern Paiute), Pueblos, and Núu-agha-tʉvʉ-pʉ (Ute) Peoples.

Chapter 10, photo 5: Ancestral lands of the Eastern Mono/Monache, Western Mono/Monache, and Numu (Northern Paiute) Peoples.

Chapter 11, photo 1: Ancestral lands of the Pueblos and Nuwuvi (Southern Paiute) Peoples.

Chapter 11, photos 2 and 3: Ancestral lands of the Nisenan Peoples.

Chapter 11, photo 4: Ancestral lands of the Nisenan Peoples.

Chapter 11, photo 5: Ancestral lands of the Chahta Yakni (Choctaw) Peoples.

Chapter 12, photo 1: Ancestral lands of the Dena'inaEłnena and Dënéndeh Peoples.

Chapter 12, photo 2: Ancestral lands of the Kluane, Dënéndeh, White River-Kluane, and Upper Tanana Peoples.

Chapter 12, photo 3: Ancestral lands of the Ahtna Nenn' and Dënéndeh Peoples.

Chapter 12, photo 4: Ancestral lands of the Dena'inaEłnena and Dënéndeh Peoples.

Chapter 12, photo 5: Ancestral lands of the Haida Peoples.

Chapter 12, photo 6: Ancestral lands of the Ahtna Nenn', Dena'inaEłnena, and Dënéndeh Peoples.

Chapter 12, photo 7: Ancestral lands of the Alutiiq (Sugpiaq) Peoples.

Chapter 12, photo 8: Ancestral lands of the Dënéndeh and Lingít Aaní (Tlingit) Peoples.

Final Thoughts, photo 1: Ancestral lands of the Dënéndeh and Tanana Peoples.

Appendices, photo 1: Ancestral lands of the Núu-agha-tu̶vu̶-pu̶ (Ute), Pueblos, and Diné Bikéyah Peoples.

Appendices, photo 2: Ancestral lands of the Alutiiq (Sugpiaq) Peoples.

Appendices, photo 3: Ancestral lands of the Dena'ina Ełnena and Dënéndeh Peoples.

Appendices, photo 4: Ancestral lands of the Ahtna Nenn' and Dënéndeh Peoples.

Appendices, photo 5: Ancestral lands of the Núu-agha-tu̶vu̶-pu̶ (Ute), Pueblos, and Nuwuvi (Southern Paiute) Peoples.

Appendices, photo 6: Ancestral lands of the Newe (Western Shoshone), Nuwuvi (Southern Paiute), and Nüwüwü (Chemehuevi) Peoples.

ABOUT THE AUTHOR

Noami J. Grevemberg is a vanlife OG (since 2016), remote entrepreneur, and dog mom living on the road in her classic Volkswagen Vanagon. Born and raised in a remote village on the island of Trinidad, she believes in nature's ability to heal and inspire. As a child, her favorite pastime was weekly poetry recitals by oil lantern in her grandmother's living room, which instilled a passion for storytelling. After leaving behind the corporate grind to live in a van full-time, Noami rekindled her love for storytelling—a gift she now uses as a tool to break down barriers and cultivate intentionally inclusive spaces. Noami is the proud founder of the Diversify Vanlife community organization, a self-taught photographer, avid outdoorist, and she considers herself an accidental minimalist. When she's not hunting for Wi-Fi or exploring the backroads of America with her partner and German Shepherd pup, you can find Noami in her tiny van kitchen cooking up fiery cultural dishes inspired by her Afro-Indo Caribbean roots.

You can follow Noami's vanlife journey on Instagram @irietoaurora or check out her website irietoaurora.com. And you can connect with the Diversify Vanlife community on Instagram @diversify.vanlife and the website diversifyvanlife.com.